PALEO DIET COOKBOOK

HEALTHY RECIPES THAT UNLOCK THE FULL POTENTIAL OF YOUR VITAMIX, BLENDTEC, NINJA, OR OTHER HIGH-SPEED, HIGH-POWER BLENDER

JAMIE BROWN

COPYRIGHT

CONTENTS

BEEF RECIPES

SNACKS RECIPES

COOKIES RECIPES

BEEF RECIPES

BEEF AND CHICKPEA KORMA

INGREDIENTS

- 1 tbsp vegetable oil
- 500g lean beef mince
- 1 brown onion, chopped
- 4cm piece fresh ginger, peeled, finely grated
- 1/3 cup korma curry paste
- 1/2 x 250g packet diced fresh pumpkin
- 2 tbsp tomato paste
- 400ml can coconut milk
- 400g can chickpeas, drained, rinsed
- 4 naan bread, warmed
- Plain Greek-style yoghurt, to serve
- Fresh mint leaves, to serve
- KACHUMBER
- 1 Lebanese cucumber, halved, seeded, thinly sliced
- 1 small red onion, finely chopped
- 1 tomato, finely chopped
- 2 tbsp lemon juice

METHOD

Step 1: Heat oil in a large frying pan over high heat. Add mince. Cook, breaking up mince with a wooden spoon, for 5 minutes or until browned. Add brown onion. Cook, stirring, for 2 minutes or until onion softens. Add ginger and curry paste. Cook, stirring, for 1 minute or until fragrant.

Step 2: Add pumpkin and tomato paste. Stir to combine. Add coconut milk and chickpeas. Bring to a simmer. Reduce heat to medium-low. Simmer for 10 to 12 minutes or until pumpkin softens.

Step 3: Meanwhile, make Kachumber: Combine cucumber, red onion, tomato and lemon juice in a small bowl. Season with salt and pepper.

Step 4: Serve curry mixture with naan, kachumber, yoghurt and mint leaves.

BEEF AND TOMATO RAGU WITH POLENTA

INGREDIENTS

- 750g pkt Coles Slow Cooked Australian Beef Ragu
- 1 1/4 cups (310ml) milk
- 2/3 cup (110g) polenta (cornmeal)
- 350g mixed medley tomatoes
- 1/2 bunch Tuscan kale, trimmed, leaves chopped

METHOD

Step 1: Prepare the beef ragu in a saucepan following packet directions.

Step 2: Meanwhile, place the milk and 2 cups (500ml) water in a large saucepan. Bring to the boil. Reduce heat to medium-low. Gradually add the polenta in a thin, steady stream, whisking constantly. Cook, stirring with a wooden spoon, for 4-5 mins or until polenta thickens. Remove from heat. Season. Cover to keep warm.

Step 3: Spray a frying pan with olive oil spray. Place over high heat. Add tomatoes. Cook, tossing gently, for 2-3 mins or until tomatoes begin to collapse. Add kale and cook, tossing gently, for 2 mins or until kale wilts slightly. Add the beef ragu. Gently stir to combine.

Step 4: Divide the polenta evenly among serving bowls. Spoon over the ragu.

BEEF SKEWERS WITH PESTO FLATBREADS

INGREDIENTS

- 1kg Coles No Added Hormones Australian Beef Blade Steak, cut into 3cm pieces
- 190g Leggo's Basil Pesto
- 1 red capsicum, seeded, halved
- 2 zucchini, thickly sliced diagonally
- 1 red onion, cut into wedges
- 1 3/4 cups (255g) self-raising flour
- 1 1/2 cups (420g) Greek-style yoghurt
- 40g baby spinach leaves
- 1 tbs olive oil

METHOD

Step 1: Thread the beef evenly onto 12 metal or soaked bamboo skewers. Brush with ¼ cup (65g) of the pesto.

Step 2: Heat a barbecue grill or chargrill on high. Cook the capsicum, skin-side down, for 5 mins or until tender. Transfer to a bowl. Cover with plastic wrap. Set aside for 5 mins to cool.

Step 3: Meanwhile, cook the zucchini and onion on the grill for 4-5 mins or until tender. Transfer to a separate bowl.

Step 4: Tear the capsicum into strips. Add to the zucchini mixture. Toss to combine.

Step 5: Place the flour and 1 cup (280g) of the yoghurt in a large bowl. Use your hands to bring the dough together. Turn onto a floured surface and gently knead until smooth. Add 2 tbs of the remaining pesto. Knead until combined. Divide dough into 4 portions. Roll each portion out on a lightly floured surface into a 5mm-thick oval. Cook on grill, in batches, for 2 mins each side or until cooked through. Transfer to a plate.

Step 6: Cook skewers on grill, turning, for 5 mins or until cooked to your liking.

Step 7: Combine remaining yoghurt and 1 tbs of remaining pesto in a bowl. Spread over the flatbreads. Top with the vegetables, spinach and skewers. Stir the oil into the remaining pesto and drizzle over the skewers. Season.

BEEF MEATBALLS WITH PITA

INGREDIENTS

- 500g Coles Australian No Added Hormones Beef 5 Star Mince
- 3/4 cup (50g) breadcrumbs (made from day-old wholegrain bread)
- 2 tsp ground cumin
- 2 garlic cloves, crushed
- 1 Coles Australian Free Range Egg, lightly whisked
- 2 tbs olive oil
- 350g pkt Coles Broccoslaw Kit salad mix
- 1 cup (160g) drained mixed marinated olives
- 250g cherry tomatoes, halved
- 4 pieces wholemeal pita bread, quartered
- 220g tzatziki dip

METHOD

Step 1: Combine the mince, breadcrumbs, cumin, garlic and egg in a large bowl. Season. Roll 1-tbs portions of mixture into balls and place on a plate. Use your hands to flatten slightly.

Step 2: Heat the oil in a large frying pan over medium heat. Add the meatballs and cook, turning occasionally, for 10 mins or until browned and cooked through. Transfer to a clean plate lined with paper towel to cool slightly.

Step 3: Just before serving, prepare salad kit in a medium bowl following packet directions. Add olives and tomato to the salad. Toss to combine. Divide the pita evenly among serving plates. Top with salad mixture and meatballs. Spoon over the tzatziki.

BEEF MADRAS TOSTADAS

INGREDIENTS

- 500g pkt Coles One Pot Beef Madras
- 2 tbs vegetable oil
- 1 brown onion, chopped
- 400g can diced tomatoes
- 4 tortillas
- 250g pkt microwavable basmati rice
- 1/2 cup shredded red cabbage
- 1/3 cup (95g) Greek-style yoghurt
- 1/4 cup coriander sprigs
- 1 long red chilli, thinly sliced (optional)

METHOD

Step 1: Preheat oven to 200°C.

Step 2: Heat a large heavy-based saucepan over medium heat. Add the beef mixture and cook, stirring, for 3-5 mins or until browned. Add the onion and cook, stirring, for 2 mins or until onion softens. Add the tomato and 2 cups (500ml) water. Bring to the boil. Reduce heat to medium-low and cook, stirring occasionally, for 1 1/2 hours or until beef is tender and sauce thickens.

Step 3: Meanwhile, line a baking tray with baking paper. Place the tortillas in a single layer on the lined tray. Spray with olive oil spray. Bake, turning once, for 6-8 mins or until light golden.

Step 4: Heat the rice following packet directions.

Step 5: Place tortillas on serving plates. Top with rice, beef mixture, cabbage, yoghurt, coriander and chilli, if using. Season.

QUICK BEEF PHO

INGREDIENTS

- 750g Coles Australian No Added Hormones Beef Rump Steak
- 4 cups (1L) Coles Vietnamese Inspired Beef Pho Stock
- 1 bunch Asian Pak Choy, quartered
- 250g rice noodles or 340g pkt Coles Asia Vermicelli Rice Noodles
- 1/3 cup coriander sprigs

METHOD

Step 1: Heat a large non-stick frying pan over high heat. Cook the beef for 2-3 mins each side for medium or until cooked to your liking. Set aside for 5 mins to rest. Thinly slice.

Step 2: Meanwhile, place the stock in a large saucepan. Bring to the boil over medium heat. Remove the pan from heat. Add the pak choy. Stir until the pak choy just wilts.

Step 3: Prepare the noodles following packet directions. Drain. Divide the noodles among serving bowls. Ladle over the broth and pak choy. Top with the beef. Sprinkle with coriander to serve.

HEALTHY BEEF STROGANOFF

INGREDIENTS

- 2 teaspoons olive oil
- 500g beef fillet, fat trimmed, thinly sliced
- 1 white onion, thinly sliced
- 200g Swiss brown mushrooms, halved or sliced
- 200g button mushrooms, halved or sliced
- 2 garlic cloves, crushed
- 1 teaspoon paprika
- 1 tablespoon Worcestershire sauce
- 200ml salt-reduced beef stock
- 60ml (1/4 cup) reduced-fat sour cream
- 100g baby spinach
- 2 x 250g pkt zucchini noodles
- Steamed green beans, to serve
- Baby parsley leaves, to serve

METHOD

Step 1: Heat half the olive oil in a large non-stick frying pan over high heat. Cook the beef, in 2 batches, for 2 minutes or until golden. Transfer to a plate.

Step 2: Heat the remaining oil in same pan over medium heat. Cook the onion, stirring, for 5 minutes or until softened. Add the mushrooms and increase heat to high. Cook, stirring, for 3-4 minutes or until browned. Add the garlic and paprika and cook, stirring, for 1 minute or until aromatic. Add the Worcestershire sauce and stock and bring to the boil.

Step 3: Reduce heat to low, return the beef to the pan and gently simmer for 1-2 minutes or until heated through. Stir through the cream and spinach and cook until spinach has just wilted.

Step 4: Microwave the zucchini noodles following packet directions. Serve the beef with the zucchini noodles and steamed green beans, and sprinkled with the parsley.

CHEAT'S BEEF LASAGNE

INGREDIENTS

- 500g Coles Australian No Added Hormones 4 Star Beef Mince
- 700g jar Coles Italian Tomato & Basil Passata
- 6 Coles Lasagne Sheets
- 490g jar bechamel sauce
- 1 cup (120g) shredded pizza cheese

METHOD

Step 1: Preheat oven to 180°C. Heat a large non-stick frying pan over medium-high heat. Add mince and cook, stirring with a wooden spoon to break up any lumps, for 5 mins or until the mince changes colour. Add the passata and stir to combine. Bring to the boil. Reduce heat to low and simmer for 10 mins or until the mince mixture thickens slightly.

Step 2: Spread one-third of the mince mixture over the base of a 6-

cup (1.5L) ovenproof dish. Top with 2 lasagne sheets, trimming to fit if necessary. Spread with one-third of the bechamel sauce and sprinkle with one-third of the cheese. Continue layering with the remaining mince mixture, lasagne sheets, bechamel sauce and cheese.

Step 3: Bake for 35 mins or until golden brown and cooked through. Set aside for 5 mins to cool slightly.

RECIPE NOTES

Allow for cooling time.

Serve with basil leaves.

Quick trick: A jar of smooth bechamel sauce is a cheat's way to add creaminess to homemade lasagne.

MOJITO BEEF TACOS

INGREDIENTS

- 1 tsp dried mint
- 1 tsp Mexican chilli powder
- 3 garlic cloves, thinly sliced
- 2 tbsp white rum
- 1/4 cup extra virgin olive oil
- 1kg piece beef rump steak
- 3 tomatoes, seeded, finely chopped
- 1/2 small red onion, finely chopped
- 1 long green chilli, seeded, finely chopped
- 1 tsp finely grated lime rind
- 1 tbsp lime juice
- 4 zucchini, peeled into ribbons
- 3 corn cobs, husks and silk removed
- 2 tbsp roughly chopped fresh mint leaves
- Small tortillas, chargrilled, to serve
- Lime wedges, to serve
- Fresh mint sprigs, to serve

METHOD

Step 1: Combine dried mint, chilli powder, garlic, rum and 1 tablespoon oil in a glass or ceramic dish. Add steak. Turn to coat. Cover. Refrigerate for 4 hours or overnight, if time permits.

Step 2: Remove steak from fridge 30 minutes before cooking and allow to come to room temperature.

Step 3: Place tomato, onion and green chilli in a serving bowl. Season. Toss to combine.

Step 4: Heat a barbecue grill on high heat. Combine lime rind, juice and remaining oil in a serving bowl. Season with salt and pepper. Grill zucchini, in batches, for 1 minute each side or until lightly charred. Transfer to lime mixture. Toss to coat. Cover to keep warm.

Step 5: Grill corn, turning, for 8 to 10 minutes or until lightly charred and tender. Transfer to a board. Stand for 5 minutes or until cool enough to handle. Cut corn kernels from cobs. Transfer to a serving bowl. Cover to keep warm.

Step 6: Grill steak for 3 minutes each side for medium-rare or until cooked to your liking. Transfer to a large plate. Cover loosely with foil. Stand for 5 minutes to rest.

Step 7: Add mint to zucchini mixture. Gently toss to combine. Thinly slice steak. Fill tortillas with steak, zucchini mixture, tomato mixture and corn. Serve with lime wedges and extra mint leaves.

BEEF POT ROAST

INGREDIENTS

- 1.5kg beef bolar blade or beef silverside roast
- 1 tbsp olive oil
- 100g pancetta slices, finely chopped
- 2 brown onions, halved, cut into thin wedges
- 1 long fresh red chilli, finely chopped
- 2 garlic cloves, crushed
- 500ml (2 cups) Tooheys Old beer
- 250ml (1 cup) passata
- 4 fresh thyme sprigs
- 2 fresh or dried bay leaves
- 2 tsp brown sugar
- 1 bunch baby carrots, peeled, trimmed
- Steamed broccolini, to serve
- Mashed potato, to serve

METHOD

Step 1: Preheat oven to 160C/180C fan forced. Place the beef on a clean chopping board. Season – this helps caramelise the meat during browning.

Step 2: Heat the oil in a large flameproof casserole dish over medium-high heat. Cook the beef, turning, for 6-8 minutes or until browned. Transfer to a plate.

Step 3: Cook the pancetta in the pan over medium heat for 1-2 minutes or until golden. Add onion, chilli and garlic and stir for 3 minutes or until soft. Return beef to pan.

Step 4: Add the beer, passata, 125ml (1/2 cup) water, thyme, bay leaves and brown sugar to the pan. Bring to the boil.

Step 5: Cover and bake, turning the beef twice 1 during cooking, for 2 /2 hours or until the beef is almost tender.

Step 6: Add carrots. Cover. Bake for 40 minutes or until beef is tender. Rest for 15 minutes. Serve with broccolini and mashed potato.

KOREAN BEEF BOWL

INGREDIENTS

- 1 1/3 cups brown rice
- 1 tbsp rice bran oil
- 1 egg, lightly beaten
- 2 garlic cloves, crushed
- 3cm piece fresh ginger, peeled, finely grated
- 500g lean beef mince
- 1/2 cup Korean BBQ bulgogi sauce and marinade
- 2 carrots
- 2 Lebanese cucumbers, thinly sliced
- 2 green onions, thinly sliced
- 2 tbsp roasted peanuts, roughly chopped
- 1/2 tsp sesame seeds
- Sriracha chilli sauce, to serve

METHOD

Step 1: Cook rice following absorption method on packet.

Step 2: Meanwhile, heat wok over medium-high heat. Add 1 teaspoon oil. Swirl to coat. Add egg. Swirl to coat base of wok. Cook, without stirring, for 1 minute or until set. Transfer to a chopping board. Roll up. Thinly slice.

Step 3: Add remaining oil to wok. Add garlic and ginger. Stir-fry for 30 seconds or until fragrant. Increase heat to high. Add mince. Cook, breaking up mince with a wooden spoon, for 6 to 8 minutes or until browned and cooked through. Add bulgogi sauce. Cook, stirring, for 2 minutes or until sauce has boiled and reduced.

Step 4: Using a julienne peeler, cut carrots into long thin strips, or thinly slice.

Step 5: Divide rice among serving bowls. Top with mince mixture, carrot, cucumber, omelette, onion, peanuts and sesame seeds. Drizzle with chilli sauce. Serve.

MEXICAN BEEF CRUNCH WRAP

INGREDIENTS

- 1/2 red capsicum
- 1/2 baby cos lettuce
- 1/2 bunch fresh coriander
- 1 tbs olive oil
- 250g beef mince
- 30g pkt taco seasoning
- 4 jumbo flour tortillas
- 110g (1 cup) pre-grated Mexican cheese blend
- 60g Doritos Nacho Cheese corn chips (about 5 chips per wrap)
- 90g (1/3 cup) thick natural yoghurt

METHOD

Step 1: Heat a large non-stick frying pan over medium-high heat. Preheat a sandwich press.

Step 2: While pan and press heat up, deseed and finely chop capsicum. Separate cos leaves. Pick coriander leaves from the stems.

Step 3: Once pan is hot, add oil. Add beef and cook, stirring, for 3 minutes or until browned. Stir in taco seasoning. Remove from heat.

Step 4: Place tortillas on a clean work surface. Divide the beef mixture among tortillas, placing in the centre. Top with cheese and corn chips in an even layer. Add the capsicum and three-quarters of the coriander. Fold in 2 opposite sides of tortillas and roll up to enclose. Place in sandwich press. Cook for 2 minutes or until golden. Serve wraps with a dollop of yoghurt, remaining coriander and cos leaves.

SLOW COOKER TERIYAKI BEEF

INGREDIENTS

- 1 tablespoon olive oil
- 1.5kg piece blade or topside beef
- 250ml (1 cup) Massel beef style liquid stock
- 80ml (1/3 cup) light soy sauce
- 60ml (1/4 cup) mirin seasoning
- 60ml (1/4 cup) cooking sake
- 2 tablespoons brown sugar
- 2 garlic cloves, crushed
- 2 teaspoons finely grated fresh ginger
- Toasted sesame seeds, to serve
- Sliced green shallots, to serve

METHOD

Step 1: Heat the oil in a large non-stick frying pan over medium-high heat. Add the beef and cook, turning often, for 10 minutes or until browned. Transfer to the slow cooker.

Step 2: Place the stock, soy sauce, mirin, sake, sugar, garlic and ginger in a jug. Stir to dissolve the sugar. Pour over the beef. Cover and cook on Low, turning the meat occasionally, for 8 hours or until very tender.

Step 3 :Transfer the beef to a large plate. Use 2 forks to coarsely shred. Return the beef to the slow cooker to cover in sauce. Divide beef among serving plates. Sprinkle with sesame seeds and shallots. Serve with sliced chilli and rice.

CHEESY BEEF AND LENTIL MEATBALLS

INGREDIENTS

- 500g lean beef mince
- 400g can brown lentils, rinsed, drained
- 1/2 red onion, finely chopped or grated
- 1 zucchini, coarsely grated
- 1/3 cup fresh basil leaves, finely chopped
- 25g (1/4 cup) quinoa flakes
- 2 garlic cloves, crushed
- 1 egg, lightly whisked
- 2 teaspoons dried oregano leaves
- 2 teaspoons olive oil
- 500ml (2 cups) tomato passata
- 200g mixed baby tomatoes, halved
- 2 teaspoons balsamic vinegar
- 40g (1/3 cup) coarsely grated fresh mozzarella
- 75g Greek feta, crumbled
- Fresh basil leaves, extra, to serve

METHOD

Step 1: Place the mince, lentils, onion, zucchini, basil, quinoa flakes, garlic, egg and 1 teaspoon of the oregano in a large bowl. Season well with salt and pepper. Use clean hands to mix well until combined. Roll rounded tablespoonfuls of the mixture into balls. Transfer to a lined plate. Cover with plastic wrap and place in the fridge for 30 minutes or until firm.

Step 2: Preheat oven to 200C/180C fan forced. Heat the oil in a large, non-stick ovenproof frying pan over medium-high heat. Cook meatballs, turning, for 8 minutes or until browned. Remove from heat. Drizzle with tomato passata, keeping meatballs slightly exposed.

Step 3: Combine tomato and vinegar in a bowl. Season. Spoon the tomato mixture among the meatballs. Sprinkle with mozzarella and feta. Sprinkle with remaining oregano. Bake for 25 minutes or until golden and bubbling. Stand for 5 minutes. Sprinkle with extra basil.

KOREAN BEEF RICE BOWL

INGREDIENTS

STEAK AND BUK CHOY

- 350g Coles beef chuck steak, sliced against the grain into 6mm thick slices, then pounded to 3mm thickness
- 2 small mandarins, zest finely chopped, juiced
- 3cm piece fresh ginger (15g), peeled, finely chopped
- 2 cloves garlic, finely chopped
- 1 birds eye chilli, finely chopped
- 1 1/2 tbsp Coles brand honey
- 1 1/2 tbsp Kikkoman soy sauce
- 1 1/2 tbsp olive oil
- 1/2 bunch baby buk choy, quartered

CARROT SALAD

- 2 small-medium carrots (160g), peeled, cut into thin matchstick-size strips
- 2 tsp Hoyt's sesame seeds, toasted
- 2 tsp Yeo's sesame Oil

TO SERVE

- 3/4 cup Coles brand long grain rice, cooked
- 1 spring onion, thinly sliced
- 4 Coles brand free range eggs, fried sunny-side up

METHOD

Step 1: To prepare the steak and buk choy, place the sliced steak in a large zip lock bag. In a medium bowl, whisk the mandarin zest, juice, ginger, garlic, chilli, honey, soy sauce, and 1 tablespoon of the oil. Coat the steak with 1 1/2 tablespoons of the marinade. Seal the bag and marinate the steak for at least 1 hour. Reserve the remaining marinade.

Step 2: Heat a char-grill pan over medium-high. In a large bowl, toss the buk choy with the remaining 1/2 tablespoon oil, season with salt, and grill for about 1 minute per side, or until grill marks form. Transfer the buk choy to a cutting board and cut out the cores. Return the buk choy to the bowl and toss with half of the reserved marinade.

Step 3: Dry the marinade off of the steak and season with salt. Increase the heat for the char-grill to high. Working in batches, grill the steak for about 30 seconds per side, or until grill marks form and the steak is cooked to medium-rare doneness. Transfer the steak to a cutting board and rest for about 2 minutes. Cut the beef into 3cm bite-size pieces and toss with the remaining reserved marinade.

Step 4: Meanwhile, to make the carrot salad and serve, in a small bowl, toss the carrot, sesame seeds, and sesame oil to coat and season with salt.

Step 5: Divide the rice among 4 bowls. Place the buk choy, carrot salad, and steak over the rice, spooning any sauce that has accumulated from the steak into the bowls. Top each with an egg, sprinkle with spring onions and serve.

RECIPE NOTES

Make-Ahead: The sliced beef can be marinated up to 1 day ahead.

BEEF STROGANOFF COB LOAF

INGREDIENTS

- 1kg beef chuck steak, excess fat trimmed
- 1 1/2 tbsp extra virgin olive oil
- 2 brown onions, thinly sliced
- 3 garlic cloves, finely chopped
- 350g cup mushrooms, sliced into thirds
- 1 tbsp sweet paprika, plus extra, to sprinkle
- 250ml (1 cup) chicken or beef stock
- 60ml (1/4 cup) passata
- 2 tbsp worcestershire sauce
- 1 tbsp dijon mustard
- 125g (1/2 cup) sour cream, plus extra, to serve
- 1 tbsp cornflour
- 1/4 cup chopped fresh continental parsley, plus extra sprigs, to serve
- 1 large cob loaf
- 60g bought garlic butter, melted

METHOD

Step 1: Slice the beef into 5 x 2cm-thick pieces. Season.

Step 2: Heat 1 tablespoon oil in a large frying pan over high heat. Cook the beef, in batches, for 5 minutes or until evenly browned. Use tongs to transfer the beef to a slow cooker.

Step 3: Heat the remaining oil in the pan. Add the onion. Reduce heat to medium. Cook, stirring often, for 5 minutes or until tender. Add the garlic and cook, stirring, for 1 minute or until aromatic. Add the mushroom and paprika. Stir to coat.

Step 4: Spoon the onion mixture over the beef in the slow cooker. Add the stock, passata, Worcestershire and Dijon. Cover and cook on High for 3 hours or until the beef is very tender.

Step 5: Place the sour cream in a bowl. Add the cornflour and about 60ml (1/4 cup) liquid from the slow cooker. Stir well to combine. Add the sour cream to the beef mixture in the slow cooker and stir to combine. Cook, stirring occasionally, for 5-10 minutes or until the sauce thickens. Stir through the parsley. Season.

Step 6: Meanwhile, preheat oven to 180C/160C fan forced. Line a baking tray with baking paper. Cut the top off the loaf, about 3cm from the top. Scoop out the bread inside, leaving a 2cm-thick shell (see note). Place the cob on prepared tray. Brush the inside of the cob with the garlic butter. Bake for 10 minutes or until golden.

Step 7: Just before serving, fill the cob shell with stroganoff. Top with extra sour cream then sprinkle with extra paprika and parsley sprigs.

RECIPE NOTES

Freeze the inside bread for breadcrumbs or cut into pieces and bake in the oven to serve with the cob.

FRENCH ONION BEEF WITH NOODLES

INGREDIENTS

- 2 tbsp extra virgin olive oil
- 25g butter
- 2 large brown onions, cut into thin wedges
- 2 garlic cloves, crushed
- 2 sprigs fresh thyme
- 500g piece beef chuck steak, trimmed
- 1/2 cup dry white wine
- 2 cups Massel Beef Style Liquid Stock
- 2 dried bay leaves
- 2 tsp brown sugar
- 150g snow peas, trimmed, halved diagonally
- 400g packet fresh thin egg noodles
- Fresh coriander sprigs, to serve

METHOD

Step 1: Heat oil and butter in a large, deep frying pan over medium heat. Add onion. Cook, stirring occasionally, for 10 to 12 minutes or until softened but not browned.

Step 2: Add garlic and thyme. Cook, stirring occasionally, for 1 minute or until fragrant. Push onion to the side of pan. Increase heat to medium-high. Add beef. Cook for 5 minutes each side, or until browned.

Step 3: Add wine. Simmer for 30 seconds. Add stock, 3 cups water and bay leaves. Season with salt and pepper. Cover. Bring to the boil. Reduce heat to low. Simmer for 3 hours, turning beef halfway during cooking, or until beef is very tender.

Step 4: Carefully transfer beef to a board and roughly shred. Return to pan. Stir in sugar. Simmer for 10 minutes. Add snow peas. Simmer for 5 minutes or until bright green and just tender.

Step 5: Divide noodles among serving bowls. Top with beef mixture. Sprinkle with coriander and green onion. Serve immediately.

BEEF POKE BOWL RECIPE

INGREDIENTS

- 1 cup (200g) jasmine rice
- 2 Coles Australian No Added Hormones Beef Scotch Fillet Steaks
- 2 limes
- 400g pkt Coles Pokeslaw Kit
- 1 avocado, stoned, peeled, sliced

METHOD

Step 1: Combine the rice and 1 1/2 cups (375ml) water in a saucepan over high heat. Bring to the boil. Reduce heat to low. Cover and cook for 10 mins or until the rice is tender and liquid is absorbed. Set aside, covered, for 5 mins to steam. Use a fork to separate the grains.

Step 2: Meanwhile, heat a greased barbecue grill or chargrill on high. Cook the steaks for 3 mins each side for medium or until cooked to your liking. Transfer to a plate and cover with foil. Set aside for 5 mins to rest. Thinly slice.

Step 3: Juice 1 lime. Place the dressing from the salad kit in a small bowl. Add the lime juice and stir to combine. Cut the remaining lime into wedges.

Step 4: Divide the rice among bowls. Top with steak, vegetable mix from the salad kit and avocado. Drizzle with dressing mixture. Sprinkle with the seed mixture from the salad kit and serve with lime wedges.

RECIPE NOTES

Allow for 5 minutes standing time and 5 minutes chilling time.

SLOW-COOKED BEEF WITH MUSHROOM

INGREDIENTS

- 4 Coles Australian No Added Hormones Beef Osso Bucco pieces
- 2 tbs plain flour
- 2 tbs olive oil
- 1 brown onion, cut into wedges
- 200g large brown flat mushrooms, thickly sliced
- 200g button mushrooms, halved
- 2 garlic cloves, crushed
- 1 cup (250ml) marsala wine or apple juice
- 2 cups (500ml) beef stock
- 4 thyme sprigs
- 2 dried bay leaves
- Steamed baby broccoli, to serve

POLENTA

- 3 cups (750ml) chicken stock
- 1 cup (250ml) milk
- 1 cup (170g) polenta (cornmeal)
- 1/2 cup (40g) finely grated parmesan
- 1/2 cup (125g) mascarpone

METHOD

Step 1: Preheat oven to 140°C. Place the beef and flour in a large bowl. Season. Toss the beef to coat.

Step 2: Heat the oil in a large flameproof roasting pan over high heat. Add the beef and cook for 2 mins each side or until the beef is golden brown. Transfer the beef to a plate.

Step 3: Add the onion, combined mushroom and garlic to the pan and cook, stirring, for 5 mins or until the onion softens. Return the beef to the pan with the wine or apple juice, stock, thyme and bay leaves. Bring to a simmer. Remove from heat.

Step 4: Cover the pan loosely with foil. Roast, turning the beef occasionally, for 2 hours or until the beef is falling off the bone and the sauce thickens slightly. Set aside, covered, for 5 mins to rest.

Step 5: Meanwhile, to make the polenta, combine the stock and milk in a large saucepan. Bring to the boil over medium-high heat. Reduce heat to medium-low. Gradually add the polenta in a thin, steady stream, whisking constantly. Cook, stirring with a wooden spoon, for 10 mins or until the polenta thickens. Remove from heat. Add parmesan and mascarpone and stir to combine. Season.

Step 6: Divide the polenta among serving bowls. Top with beef and spoon over the sauce. Serve with baby broccoli.

RECIPE NOTES

In a slow cooker

Prepare the beef mixture in a large, deep frying pan, then transfer to a slow cooker. Cover and cook for 4 hours on high (or 6 hours on low).

SLOW COOKED BEEF AND POTATOES

INGREDIENTS

- 900g Coles Australian No Added Hormones Beef Chuck Steak, halved crossways
- 2 tbs plain flour
- 1 tbs olive oil
- 1 brown onion, thinly sliced
- 4 bacon rashers, chopped
- 1 cup (250ml) beef stock
- 1/4 cup (60ml) balsamic vinegar
- 3 medium white potatoes, chopped
- 60g pkt Coles Australian Baby Spinach
- Coles Bakery Stone Baked by Laurent Sourdough Vienna, sliced, toasted, to serve

METHOD

Step 1: Preheat oven to 160°C. Place the beef and flour in a bowl. Toss until beef is well coated, shaking off excess.

Step 2: Heat the oil in a large ovenproof frying pan over high heat. Cook beef for 3 mins each side or until browned. Transfer to a plate.

Step 3: Add the onion and bacon to the pan and cook, stirring, for 3 mins or until onion softens slightly. Return the beef to the pan with any juices on the plate. Add the stock and vinegar. Bring to the boil. Add the potato. Season. Cover and bake for 1 hour. Uncover and cook for a further 30 mins or the beef is tender and the sauce thickens slightly.

Step 4: Add the spinach to the beef mixture in the pan and gently fold to combine. Serve with the bread.

TRADITIONAL ROAST BEEF
WITH VEG

INGREDIENTS

- 1.3kg Coles Australian No Added Hormones Beef Roast Topside
- 1kg baby white potatoes, halved or quartered
- 450g gold sweet potato, peeled, coarsely chopped
- 1/3 cup (80ml) extra virgin olive oil
- 200g green beans, trimmed
- 1 tbs chopped basil
- 1 tbs chopped flat-leaf parsley
- 1 garlic clove, crushed

METHOD

Step 1: Preheat oven to 250°C. Line a large roasting pan with baking paper. Arrange beef, potato and sweet potato in lined pan. Drizzle with half the oil, turning vegetables to coat. Season.

Roast beef step 01

Step 2: Reduce oven to 200°C. Roast, turning the vegetables once, for 1 hour (or until the internal temperature of the beef is 60-65°C) for medium or until beef is cooked to your liking. Cover with foil. Rest for 10 mins.

Step 3: Meanwhile, place beans in a heatproof bowl and cover with boiling water. Set aside for 2 mins or until just tender. Drain well. Combine the basil, parsley, garlic and remaining oil in a small bowl.

Step 4: Drizzle beef with the basil mixture. Serve with the beans and vegetables.

RECIPE NOTES

Allow for 10 minutes resting time.

TIMER TIP: Roast the beef for 15-20 mins per 500g for rare, 20-25 mins per 500g for medium and 25-30 mins per 500g for well-done.

Leftovers idea: Cold roast beef is great in salads and sandwiches the next day. Try this tasty salad recipe for 4 to use up any leftovers.

MEXICAN BEEF STEW WITH BEANS

INGREDIENTS

- 1 large dried chipotle chilli (see tip)
- 1.2kg grass-fed beef chuck steak or gravy beef, excess fat trimmed, left in large pieces
- 60ml (1/4 cup) extra virgin olive oil
- 2 red onions, sliced
- 2 red capsicums, deseeded, chopped
- 2 celery sticks, thinly sliced
- 3 teaspoons cumin seeds
- 2 teaspoons coriander seeds
- 2 x 400g cans whole peeled tomatoes
- 400g can black beans or kidney beans, rinsed, drained
- 500ml (2 cups) Massel Beef Style Liquid Stock
- 2 garlic cloves, chopped
- 1 cinnamon stick
- 2 corncobs, chargrilled, sliced
- Natural yoghurt, to serve
- Dried chilli flakes, to serve (optional)

METHOD

Step 1: Preheat oven to 140°C/120°C fan forced. Place chipotle chilli in a heatproof bowl. Cover with boiling water and set aside for 10 minutes to soak.

Step 2: Meanwhile, season beef. Heat half the oil in a large flameproof casserole dish over medium-high heat. Cook beef, in batches, for 2 minutes each side or until golden. Use slotted spoon to transfer to heatproof bowl.

Step 3: Reduce heat to medium. Pour remaining oil into dish. Add the onion, capsicum and celery. Cook, stirring, for 5 minutes or until light golden.

Step 4: Meanwhile, place the cumin and coriander seeds in a mortar and pound with a pestle until finely crushed. Drain chipotle chilli and coarsely chop.

Step 5: Add the tomatoes, beans, stock, garlic, cinnamon, chipotle and cumin mixture to dish. Return beef to dish with any juices. Bring to boil. Cover. Bake for 3 1/2 hours or until mixture thickens and beef is falling apart.

Step 6: Use a fork to shred beef into large chunks. Top the stew with the corn, yoghurt or sour cream, coriander sprigs and chilli flakes, if using. Season and serve.

RECIPE NOTES

If dried chipotle is unavailable, use 1 tsp chipotle in adobo sauce from a jar instead.

SLOW-COOKED BEEF MOUSSAKA

INGREDIENTS

- 750g Coles Australian No Added Hormones Gravy Beef, cut into 3cm pieces
- 2 tbs plain flour
- 1 tbs olive oil
- 1 brown onion, finely chopped
- 2 celery sticks, thinly sliced
- 2 garlic cloves, crushed
- 690g Coles Italian Passata
- 1/2 cup (140g) tomato paste
- 1 tsp caster sugar
- 2 tbs chopped oregano
- 1 medium eggplant, sliced crossways
- 375g smooth ricotta
- 2 tbs buttermilk
- 1/2 cup (40g) finely grated parmesan
- 1/4 tsp ground paprika
- Oregano sprigs, to serve

METHOD

Step 1: Place the beef and flour in a large bowl and toss to combine. Heat the oil in a large frying pan over high heat.

Step 2: Cook the beef, in 3 batches, turning occasionally, for 5 mins or until brown all over. Transfer to a slow cooker.

Step 3: Add the onion, celery, garlic, passata, tomato paste and sugar to the slow cooker. Stir to combine. Season. Cover and cook for 4 hours on high (or 6 hours on low) or until beef is very tender. Stir in the chopped oregano.

Step 4: Meanwhile, preheat grill on high. Spray a baking tray with olive oil spray. Place the eggplant slices on the tray. Spray with olive oil spray. Cook under the grill for 2 mins each side or until the eggplant is lightly browned and tender.

Step 5: Arrange the eggplant slices over the beef mixture in the slow cooker. Place the ricotta, buttermilk and parmesan in a bowl and stir until smooth. Season. Spoon ricotta mixture evenly over the eggplant in the slow cooker. Sprinkle with paprika. Cover and cook for 30 mins on high (or 1 hour on low) or until heated through.

Step 6: Sprinkle the moussaka with oregano sprigs to serve.

PEPPERED BEEF PANZANELLA SALAD

INGREDIENTS

- 2 garlic cloves, crushed
- 1/4 cup (60ml) olive oil
- 250g Coles Finest By Laurent Sourdough Baguette*, cut into 4cm pieces
- 1 yellow capsicum, seeded, coarsely chopped
- 600g Coles Australian No Added Hormones Beef Rump Steak
- 2 tsp coarsely ground peppercorns
- 250g cherry tomatoes, halved
- 1 Lebanese cucumber, coarsely chopped
- 1/2 red onion, thinly sliced
- 3/4 cup (115g) pitted kalamata olives
- 2 tbs Coles Italian White Wine Vinegar
- 1/3 cup (25g) shaved parmesan
- 1/2 cup basil leaves, torn

METHOD

Step 1: Combine the garlic and 1 tbs oil in a bowl. Add bread and toss to coat.

Step 2: Heat a barbecue grill or chargrill on medium-high. Cook the bread and capsicum, turning, for 4-5 mins or until the bread is crisp and the capsicum is lightly charred. Transfer to a plate.

Step 3: Rub beef with 1 tbs oil and sprinkle with the pepper. Cook beef for 3 mins each side or until cooked to your liking. Transfer to a plate and cover with foil. Set aside for 5 mins to rest. Thinly slice.

Step 4: Meanwhile, combine the tomato, cucumber, onion and olives in a bowl. Whisk vinegar and remaining oil in a small bowl. Season. Add to the tomato mixture with beef and bread mixture. Toss to combine. Transfer to a serving platter. Top with parmesan and basil.

THAI MASSAMAN BEEF SALAD

INGREDIENTS

- 1/4 cup massaman curry paste
- 2cm piece fresh ginger, finely grated
- 2 garlic cloves, crushed
- 1/2 lemongrass stalk, white part only, very finely chopped
- 600g beef rump steak, trimmed
- 2 tablespoons sweet chilli sauce
- 2 tablespoons white vinegar
- 3 baby cucumbers, thinly sliced into rounds
- 400g chat potatoes
- 1 tablespoon peanut oil
- 2 teaspoons tamarind puree
- 2 teaspoons brown sugar
- 2 teaspoons fish sauce
- 2 teaspoons crunchy peanut butter
- 270ml can light coconut milk
- 120g mixed salad leaves
- 200g tomato medley, sliced
- 1 small red onion, thinly sliced into rounds

- 1/2 cup fresh coriander leaves
- 1/3 cup fresh Thai basil leaves
- 1/4 cup fresh mint leaves
- 1 cup bean sprouts, trimmed
- 1/4 cup roughly chopped roasted peanuts

METHOD

Step 1: Combine 2 tablespoons curry paste with 1 tablespoon water, ginger, garlic and lemongrass. Place beef in a shallow glass or ceramic dish. Rub all over with paste mixture. Cover. Refrigerate for 3 hours or overnight.

Step 2: Meanwhile, combine chilli sauce and vinegar in a glass bowl. Add cucumber. Season. Cover. Set aside for 2 hours.

Step 3: Place potatoes in a large saucepan. Cover with cold water. Bring to the boil over high heat. Reduce heat to medium. Boil for 10 to 12 minutes or until just tender. Drain. Cool for 15 minutes. Slice thickly. Drizzle with peanut oil. Season with salt and pepper.

Step 4: Heat a large chargrill pan on medium-high heat. Cook potato slices, in batches, for 2 to 3 minutes or until charred. Transfer to a plate. Cook steak for 3 to 4 minutes each side, for medium, or until cooked to your liking. Transfer to a plate. Cover loosely with foil. Set aside for 5 minutes to rest.

Step 5: Meanwhile, cook remaining curry paste in a small saucepan over medium-high heat for 2 minutes. Add tamarind puree, sugar, sh sauce, peanut butter and coconut milk. Bring to a simmer. Reduce heat to medium. Simmer, stirring occasionally, for 4 to 5 minutes or until sauce thickens.

Step 6: Arrange salad leaves, potato, tomato, onion, herbs, bean sprouts and cucumber on a large platter. Slice beef. Place on top of salad. Drizzle with tamarind sauce and sprinkle with peanuts. Serve.

HAYDEN QUINN'S REEF AND BEEF

INGREDIENTS

- 1-kilogram beef rib eye steak, on the bone
- 2 tbsp sea salt
- MUSHROOMS
- 3 king oyster mushrooms, halved
- 1 tbsp Cobram Estate Extra Virgin Olive oil
- ABALONE
- 1 tbsp unsalted butter
- 1 tbsp Cobram Estate Extra Virgin Olive Oil
- 1 greenlip abalone, cleaned and tenderised, thinly sliced
- 1 garlic clove, finely chopped
- 1 tbsp fresh continental parsley, finely chopped

METHOD

Step 1: Remove the steak from the fridge and allow to come to room temperature for cooking. Preheat your Weber barbecue over high heat with the lid down so the grill bars are super hot for cooking. Season steak well on both sides with sea salt. Place the steak on the grill and cook for 20-25 minutes, or until cooked to your liking (see notes).

Step 2: Meanwhile, brush the mushrooms with olive oil and place on the barbecue. Cook until softened and slightly charred.

Step 3: For the abalone, heat a heavy-based frying pan over high heat. Add butter and olive oil and cook until butter has melted. Add the abalone and garlic. Stir-fry quickly for 1-2 minutes or until abalone is just cooked. Remove from heat and toss through the parsley. Season with sea salt.

Step 4: Divide the steak, mushrooms and abalone among serving plates.

RECIPE NOTES

Be sure to monitor the steak with meat thermometer. For medium-rare, remove the steak from the grill once it reaches an internal temperature of 50°C, then allow it to rest up to 55°C

Abalone can be substituted for green prawns

SLOW COOKER MONGOLIAN BEEF

INGREDIENTS

- 60ml (1/4 cup) light soy sauce
- 60ml (1/4 cup) Chinese cooking wine
- 1 1/2 tbsp cornflour
- 1.2kg beef chuck steak, excess fat trimmed, cut into 2-3cm pieces
- 2 tbsp peanut oil
- 3 garlic cloves, finely chopped
- 1 tbsp finely shredded fresh ginger
- 60ml (1/4 cup) oyster sauce
- 2 tsp caster sugar
- 1 tsp Massel Chicken Stock Powder
- 2 carrots, peeled, halved lengthways, sliced
- White pepper, to season
- Cooked egg noodles, to serve
- Sesame oil, to serve
- Thinly sliced long fresh red chilli, to serve
- Fresh coriander sprigs, to serve

METHOD

Step 1: Place the soy sauce, cooking wine and cornflour in a large bowl. Stir until combined. Add the beef and stir to coat. Cover and set aside for 20 minutes to marinate.

Step 2: Heat half the peanut oil in a large non-stick frying pan over high heat. Drain beef, reserving marinade. Add half the beef to pan and cook, turning occasionally, for 5 minutes or until browned. Transfer to a slow cooker. Repeat with the remaining peanut oil and beef.

Step 3: Add the garlic and ginger to the pan. Cook, stirring, for 1 minute or until aromatic. Add oyster sauce, sugar, stock powder, reserved marinade and 250ml (1 cup) water. Stir to combine. Pour into the slow cooker. Cover and cook on High for 4 hours or until the beef is very tender, adding the carrot in the last 2 hours of cooking. Season with salt and white pepper.

Step 4: Place noodles in serving bowls. Divide the Mongolian beef among the bowls. Drizzle over sesame oil and top with chilli and coriander to serve.

LOADED CAJUN BEEF

INGREDIENTS

- 539g pkt frozen sweet potato crinkle-cut chips
- 1 ripe tomato, finely chopped
- 125g can corn kernels, drained
- 1 avocado, finely chopped
- 1/4 cup chopped fresh coriander leaves
- 1 red onion, finely chopped
- 1 tablespoon olive oil
- 500g lean beef mince
- 1 1/2 tablespoons Cajun seasoning
- Sour cream, to serve
- Lime wedges, to serve

METHOD

Step 1: BAKE THE CHIPS & MAKE THE SALSA Preheat the oven to 220C/200C fan forced. Place sweet potato chips in a single layer on a large baking tray. Bake, turning halfway, for 20 minutes or until tender. Combine the tomato, corn, avocado, coriander and half the onion in a bowl. Season. Toss to combine.

Step 2: COOK THE MINCE Meanwhile, heat the oil in a large frying pan over high heat. Add the remaining onion and cook for 1-2 minutes. Add the mince and Cajun seasoning. Cook, stirring with a wooden spoon to break up the mince, for 6 minutes or until browned. Add 80ml (1/3 cup) water and cook for a further 1-2 minutes. Remove from the heat.

Step 3: TIME TO SERVE Arrange the sweet potato chips and mince mixture on a serving platter. Top with the avocado salsa and dollops of sour cream. Serve with lime wedges.

BEEF AND BEAN TACOS

INGREDIENTS

- 500g Cook with Curtis Mexican Recipe Beef Mince
- 2 tsp plain flour
- 454g can refried beans, warmed
- 8 corn or small flour tortillas, warmed
- Shredded lettuce, to serve
- Tomato wedges, to serve

METHOD

Step 1: Heat a large non-stick frying pan over high heat. Add beef and cook, stirring to break up lumps, for 3 mins or until cooked through.

Step 2: Stir in flour, then stir in 1/3 cup (80ml) water and cook for 2 mins or until sauce thickens slightly and coats beef. Season with salt.

Step 3: Spoon beans over tortillas and top with the beef mixture, lettuce and tomato wedges.

JAPANESE BEEF CURRY

INGREDIENTS

- 20g butter
- 2 teaspoons olive oil
- 1kg chuck beef steak, cut into 3-4cm pieces
- 1 brown onion, cut into thin wedges
- 3 teaspoons finely grated fresh ginger
- 3 garlic cloves, finely chopped
- 2 tablespoons madras curry powder
- 40g (1/4 cup) plain flour
- 3 potatoes, peeled, coarsely chopped
- 1 large carrot, peeled, coarsely chopped
- 1 green apple, cored, coarsely grated
- 1 tablespoon tomato sauce
- 1 tablespoon Worcestershire sauce
- 1 tablespoon light soy sauce
- 1 teaspoon garam masala
- Steamed sushi rice, to serve
- Toasted sesame seeds, to sprinkle (optional)
- Quick vegetable pickle, to serve (optional)

METHOD

Step 1: Heat the oil and the butter in a large casserole dish over high heat. Season the beef and cook, in 2-3 batches, for 5 minutes each batch or until browned. Use tongs to transfer to a plate.

Step 2: Reduce the heat to low. Add the onion to the dish and cook, stirring often, for 5 minutes or until golden. Add the ginger and garlic. Cook, stirring, for 1 minute or until aromatic. Stir in the curry powder.

Step 3: Increase the heat to high. Return the beef to the dish. Stir to combine. Sprinkle over the flour and stir well to coat. Add 750ml (3 cups) water and stir, scraping the bottom of the dish with a wooden spoon, until the mixture is smooth. Add the potato, carrot and apple. Bring to the boil. Reduce heat to low and cover. Simmer for 2 hours or until the beef is very tender. Remove from heat.

Step 4: Stir in the tomato sauce, Worcestershire, soy sauce and garam masala. Season. Set aside for 10 minutes to rest. Serve the curry with steamed rice and sprinkled with sesame seeds, if using. A quick pickle is a terrific condiment.

MINI BEEF WELLINGTONS

INGREDIENTS

- 2 French shallots, peeled, coarsely chopped
- 40g butter, chopped
- 300g portobello mushrooms, wiped clean, chopped
- 2 tsp fresh thyme leaves
- 1 tbsp pâté
- 200g baby spinach, coarsely chopped
- 1 tbsp olive oil
- 400g beef eye fillet
- 100g prosciutto slices
- 1 tbsp Dijon mustard
- 2 sheets frozen butter puff pastry, just thawed
- 1 egg, lightly whisked
- Caramelised onion relish, to serve

METHOD

Step 1: Place shallot in a food processor. Process until finely chopped. Place butter in a frying pan over medium heat and melt until foaming. Add shallot. Cook for 3 minutes or until softened. Meanwhile, process mushroom until finely chopped. Add to pan. Cook for 8-10 minutes or until liquid has evaporated. Stir in thyme and pâté. Transfer to a plate. Set aside to cool completely.

Step 2: Heat a non-stick frying pan over medium heat. Add spinach. Cook for 2-3 minutes or until wilted. Remove from pan and set aside to cool. Wipe pan clean and place over high heat. Season beef well. Spray pan with oil and sear beef for 30 seconds each side. (Be careful not to overcook beef at this stage.) Transfer to a plate and pat dry. Place in the fridge for 30 minutes to chill. Use hands to squeeze any excess liquid from spinach.

Step 3: Place a pastry sheet on a larger square of plastic wrap. Top with half the prosciutto, overlapping, to cover pastry. Spread half the mushroom mixture down centre. Top with half the spinach. Slice beef lengthways to make 2 long pieces. Place 1-piece on top of spinach. Spread with half the mustard. Use plastic wrap to roll up tightly from 1 long edge of pastry like a bonbon. Repeat with remaining pastry, prosciutto, mushroom mixture, spinach, beef and mustard to make another Wellington. Place both Wellingtons in the freezer overnight to freeze.

Step 4: Preheat oven to 220C/200C fan forced. Grease a baking tray and line with baking paper. Unwrap frozen Wellingtons and place, seam-side down, on prepared tray. Brush with egg. Bake for 40-45 minutes or until pastry is golden and crispy. Set aside for 10 minutes to rest. Slice and serve warm with relish.

RECIPE NOTES

Make ahead up to the end of step 3 and freeze for up to 3 months. Continue with step 4 just before serving.

Cooks best from frozen.

EASY BEEF STIR-FRY

INGREDIENTS

- 2 x 300g pkts Coles Made Easy Beef Stir Fry Strips in Thai Seasoning*
- 2 x 300g pkts Coles Australian Superfood Stir-Fry
- 450g pkt microwavable jasmine rice
- 1 cup (150g) dry-roasted cashews
- 1 cup coriander sprigs

METHOD

Step 1: Heat a wok or large non-stick frying pan over high heat. Add one-quarter of the beef. Stir-fry for 1-2 mins or until just cooked through. Transfer to a plate. Repeat, in 3 more batches, with the remaining beef.

Step 2: Return the beef to the wok or pan with the vegetables and 1 cup (250ml) water. Stir-fry for 2-3 mins or until just heated through.

Step 3: Heat the rice in microwave following packet directions. Divide among serving bowls. Top with the beef mixture. Sprinkle with cashews and coriander to serve.

SATAY BEEF AND NOODLE STIR-FRY

INGREDIENTS

- 3 x 70g bundles plain instant noodles
- 1/4 cup smooth peanut butter
- 2 tablespoons oyster sauce
- 1/3 cup boiling water
- 1 1/2 tablespoons vegetable oil
- 400g beef rump steak, trimmed, sliced
- 1 red onion, halved, sliced
- 2 garlic cloves, crushed
- 1/2 bunch kale, stems removed, leaves roughly shredded
- 227g can sliced water chestnuts, drained
- 2 tablespoons chopped roasted salted peanuts
- 1 tablespoon sesame seeds, toasted
- 1 Lebanese cucumber, halved lengthways, sliced

METHOD

Step 1: Cook noodles following packet directions. Drain. Rinse under cold water to cool. Drain well.

Step 2: Meanwhile, combine peanut butter, oyster sauce and boiling water in a small bowl.

Step 3: Heat 1 teaspoon oil in a wok or large frying pan over high heat. Season beef with salt. Add 1/2 the beef, making sure it's in a single layer. Cook, without stirring, for 30 seconds. Stir-fry and transfer to a plate (see note). Repeat with 1 teaspoon oil and remaining beef.

Step 4: Heat 2 teaspoons oil in pan. Add onion. Stir-fry for 3 minutes. Add garlic. Stir, then transfer onion mixture to a large bowl. Heat remaining oil in pan. Add kale and water chestnuts. Stir-fry for 2 minutes. Return onion mixture to pan with peanut butter mixture and noodles. Stir-fry over medium-low heat until well combined. Toss through beef with any resting juices. Sprinkle with peanut and sesame seeds. Serve with cucumber.

RECIPE NOTES

To keep beef tender, cook in 2 batches in a very hot pan. Place in a single layer in pan and avoid stirring for good browning and flavour.

TEX-MEX PULLED BEEF TACOS

INGREDIENTS

TEXAN-STYLE PULLED BEEF

- 2 tsp olive oil
- 1.5kg Coles Australian No Added Hormones Beef Brisket
- 2 brown onions, cut into wedges
- 2 cups (500ml) beef or chicken stock
- 1/4 cup (60ml) apple cider vinegar
- 2 garlic cloves, crushed
- 2 tbs maple syrup
- 1 tbs Worcestershire sauce
- 1 tbs tomato sauce
- 1 tbs Dijon or American mustard
- 2 tsp smoked paprika
- 1 tsp onion salt
- 1 tsp garlic powder
- 2 tsp dried oregano
- 1 tsp ground cumin

TEX-MEX PULLED BEEF TACOS

- ½ quantity Texan-Style Pulled Beef (above)
- 1 tbs taco seasoning
- 12 small soft tortillas
- 1/4 small red cabbage, finely shredded
- 1/4 small savoy cabbage, finely shredded
- 1 avocado, stoned, peeled, thinly sliced
- 1 carrot, peeled, cut into matchsticks
- 1/2 cup (120g) sour cream
- 2 tsp sriracha or chilli sauce
- 1/2 cup (130g) tomato salsa
- Drained sliced jalapeños, to serve
- Coriander leaves, to serve
- Lime wedges, to serve

METHOD

Step 1: To make the pulled beef, preheat oven to 150°C. Heat oil in a frying pan over high heat. Season beef. Cook beef in pan for 5 mins each side or until golden. Transfer to a roasting pan.

Step 2: Arrange onion around the beef in the pan. Whisk stock, vinegar, garlic, maple syrup, Worcestershire sauce, tomato sauce, mustard, paprika, onion salt, garlic powder, oregano and cumin in a jug. Pour evenly over beef, turning to coat.

Step 3: Cover pan tightly with foil. Roast for 3 hours or until beef is very tender and falls apart when tested with a fork. Increase oven to 180°C. Uncover and roast for a further 30 mins or until beef is golden brown and sauce thickens slightly. Set aside for 15 mins to rest.

Step 4: Use 2 forks to coarsely shred beef. Stir to combine with pan juices. Season.

Step 5: To make the tacos, heat a large frying pan over high heat. Add the beef and taco seasoning. Cook, stirring, for 5 mins or until heated through.

Step 6: Heat a chargrill on high. Cook the tortillas, in 4 batches, for 1 min each side or until lightly charred. Transfer to a plate.

Step 7: Divide the tortillas among serving plates. Top with combined cabbage, avocado, carrot and beef mixture.

Step 8: Combine the sour cream and sriracha or chilli sauce in a small bowl.

Step 9: Spoon the cream mixture over the tacos and top with salsa. Sprinkle with jalapeños and coriander. Serve with lime wedges.

RECIPE NOTES

STEP-BY-STEP PULLED BEEF

Brown the meat - For richer-tasting pulled beef, brown the beef in a frying pan before slow-cooking it in the oven. Not only does this seal in the juices and keep the beef tender, but it also creates a caramelised crust that tastes delicious.

Pour in the liquid - Adding stock mixture to the pan boosts the flavour. The liquid will also turn to steam as it heats in the oven, which cooks the beef evenly and keeps it juicy and tender. This makes the beef easier to shred at the end of cooking.

Cover it tightly - To trap the liquid in the pan, cover the pan tightly with foil. This creates steam, which cooks the beef and makes it meltingly tender. If steam escapes, the liquid evaporates too quickly and the beef becomes too dry to shred.

Get ready to shred - For a great-tasting finish, you want even-sized pieces of beef well-coated in the sauce. Use 2 forks to shred the beef along the grain. Forks are the best utensils for pulling beef as the prongs will finely and evenly tear away meat.

BEEF BRISKET WITH PARSLEY-LEMON POTATOES

INGREDIENTS

- 1.2kg Coles Australian No Added Hormones Beef Brisket
- 1 tbs olive oil
- 1 brown onion, coarsely chopped
- 1 fennel, trimmed, coarsely chopped
- 6 garlic cloves, crushed
- 1 1/2 tbs tomato paste
- 3 cups (750ml) salt-reduced beef stock
- 1 cup (250ml) dry white wine
- 750g Carisma or washed potatoes
- 2 tbs extra virgin olive oil
- 2 tbs finely chopped parsley
- 1 lemon, rind finely grated, juiced
- 2 tsp plain flour

METHOD

Step 1: Preheat oven to 150°C (130°C fan-forced). Season the brisket with salt and pepper. In a large ovenproof casserole pan over medium-high heat, heat the olive oil. Cook the brisket for 5 mins each side or until browned. Transfer to a plate and set aside to rest.

Step 2: If necessary, pour off all but 1 tbs oil from the pan. Add the onion, fennel and garlic and cook, stirring, for 8 mins or until just tender. Reduce heat to medium. Add the tomato paste and cook, stirring frequently, for 2 mins or until the tomato paste deepens in colour. Add stock and wine, scraping the bottom of the pan. Return the brisket, fat-side up, to the pan and bring to a simmer. Cover and transfer to the oven. Braise for 3 hours or until very tender.

Step 3: Increase oven temperature to 200°C (180°C fan-forced). Uncover brisket and cook for 1 hour or until brisket is crisp on top and the liquid has reduced by about half. Transfer the brisket to a carving board. Cover with foil. Strain the braising liquid through a fine sieve into a heatproof jug, pressing on the vegetables to extract liquid. Set the brisket aside for 30 mins to rest.

Step 4: While the brisket is resting, in a large saucepan, add the potatoes, 1 tbs salt and enough water to cover. Bring to a boil over medium-high heat. Reduce heat to low and simmer for 30-35 mins or until the potatoes are tender. Drain well and return to the pan. Using a fork, crush the potatoes into large chunks. Fold in the extra virgin olive oil, parsley, lemon rind and 1 tbs lemon juice. Season. Cover to keep warm.

Step 5: Skim off as much fat as possible from the braising liquid in jug. Wipe out the casserole pan and add the braising liquid. (You'll need 2 cups/500ml of braising liquid. Top up with more beef stock if necessary.) Bring to the boil over medium-high heat. In a small bowl, combine the flour with 1/4 cup (60ml) of the braising liquid from the pan until completely smooth. Add the flour mixture to the pan, whisking to combine. Return to the boil and cook for 1 min or until the gravy thickens slightly. Remove from heat. Season.

Step 6: Slice the brisket against the grain into 1cm-thick slices. Return the sliced brisket to the gravy in the pan. Cover and set aside for 10 mins to rest.

Step 7: Arrange the potato mixture on a large serving platter. Top the potato mixture with the sliced brisket and drizzle with the gravy.

RECIPE NOTES

Allow for resting time.

Serve with: chopped parsley and lemon zest.

GET AHEAD: The brisket can be made up to 2 days ahead. After slicing, allow to cool in gravy then refrigerate in an airtight container.

MONGOLIAN-STYLE BEEF
RICE BOWL

INGREDIENTS

- 1 1/2 cups (300g) sushi rice, rinsed, drained
- 2 spring onions, cut into matchsticks
- 500g Coles Australian No Added Hormones 4 Star Beef Mince
- 2 tsp finely grated ginger
- 1 tsp Chinese five spice
- 1/3 cup (80ml) oyster sauce
- 1/4 cup (60ml) hoisin sauce
- 1 bunch baby buk choy, trimmed, halved lengthways
- 2 carrots, peeled, cut into long matchsticks
- 2 tbs peanuts, chopped

METHOD

Step 1: Place the rice and 2 1/4 cups (560ml) cold water in a large saucepan over high heat. Bring to the boil. Reduce heat to low. Cover and cook for 12 mins or until the rice is tender and the water is absorbed. Set aside, covered, for 5 mins to steam.

Step 2: Meanwhile, place the spring onion in a small bowl and cover with iced water. Set aside for 10 mins to curl.

Step 3: Heat a wok or large frying pan over high heat. Add the mince and cook, stirring with a wooden spoon to break up lumps, for 5 mins or until the mince changes colour. Add the ginger and five spice and stir-fry for 1 min or until aromatic. Add the oyster sauce and hoisin sauce and stir-fry for 2-3 mins or until heated through.

Step 4: Place the buk choy in a large heatproof bowl. Pour over boiling water. Set aside for 1 min or until just tender. Refresh under cold water. Drain well.

Step 5: Drain spring onion curls. Divide rice among serving bowls. Top with mince mixture, carrot, spring onion curls and buk choy. Sprinkle with peanut.

RECIPE NOTES

Serve with: sliced red chilli and coriander sprigs

SWAP ME: We use beef mince in this recipe, but you can use pork mince instead or a mixture

of the two.

JACKET POTATOES WITH TEXAN-STYLE BEEF

INGREDIENTS

- 6 large brushed potatoes, scrubbed
- 1/4 quantity Texan-Style Pulled Beef (below)
- 1/2 x 400g can black beans, rinsed, drained
- 1/2 cup (60g) coarsely grated cheddar
- 1 vine-ripened tomato, finely chopped
- 1/2 red onion, finely chopped
- 2 tbs finely chopped chives
- Mint leaves, to serve

TEXAN-STYLE PULLED BEEF

- 2 tsp olive oil
- 1.5kg Coles Australian No Added Hormones Beef Brisket
- 2 brown onions, cut into wedges
- 2 cups (500ml) beef or chicken stock
- 1/4 cup (60ml) apple cider vinegar

- 2 garlic cloves, crushed
- 2 tbs maple syrup
- 1 tbs Worcestershire sauce
- 1 tbs tomato sauce
- 1 tbs Dijon or American mustard
- 2 tsp smoked paprika
- 1 tsp onion salt
- 1 tsp garlic powder
- 2 tsp dried oregano
- 1 tsp ground cumin

METHOD

Step 1: To make the Texan-style pulled beef, preheat oven to 150°C. Heat oil in a frying pan over high heat. Season beef. Cook beef in pan for 5 mins each side or until golden. Transfer to a roasting pan.

Step 2: Arrange onion around the beef in the pan. Whisk stock, vinegar, garlic, maple syrup, Worcestershire sauce, tomato sauce, mustard, paprika, onion salt, garlic powder, oregano and cumin in a jug. Pour evenly over beef, turning to coat.

Step 3: Cover pan tightly with foil. Roast for 3 hours or until beef is very tender and falls apart when tested with a fork. Increase oven to 180°C. Uncover and roast for a further 30 mins or until beef is golden brown and sauce thickens slightly. Set aside for 15 mins to rest.

Step 4: Use 2 forks to coarsely shred beef. Stir to combine with pan juices. Season.

Step 5: To make the jacket potatoes, preheat oven to 180°C. Prick potatoes all over with a fork. Wrap each potato in foil and place on a baking tray. Bake for 1 hour or until tender. Unwrap potatoes and bake for a further 10 mins or until light golden. Set aside to cool slightly.

Step 6: Meanwhile, combine beef and beans in a small saucepan over low heat. Cook for 5 mins or until heated through.

Step 7: Use a sharp knife to cut a cross in top of each potato and gently squeeze base to open. Top with beef mixture and sprinkle with cheddar. Bake for 5 mins or until cheddar melts.

Step 8: Combine tomato and onion in a bowl. Divide potatoes among serving plates. Top with tomato mixture, chive and mint.

MOROCCAN-STYLE BEEF WITH JEWELLED COUSCOUS

INGREDIENTS

- 4 (about 150g each) Coles Australian No Added Hormones Beef Rump Steaks
- 2 tbs olive oil
- 1 tbs Moroccan seasoning
- 1 1/4 cups (250g) wholemeal couscous
- 1/4 cup (40g) finely chopped pitted fresh dates
- 1/4 cup (40g) chopped dried apricots
- 1 1/4 cups (310ml) boiling water
- 1/4 cup (35g) slivered almonds, toasted
- 2 tbs lemon juice
- 60g pkt Coles Australian Baby Rocket
- 1/3 cup mint leaves

METHOD

Step 1: Heat a chargrill on medium-high. Rub steaks with half the oil and sprinkle with the Moroccan seasoning. Cook for 3-4 mins each side for medium or until cooked to your liking. Transfer to a plate and cover with foil to keep warm.

Step 2: Meanwhile, place the couscous in a heatproof bowl. Add the date and apricot and stir to combine. Stir in the boiling water. Cover with plastic wrap and set aside for 4-5 mins or until the liquid is absorbed. Use a fork to separate the grains.

Step 3: Add the almond, lemon juice and remaining oil to the couscous mixture and stir to combine. Season.

Step 4: Thickly slice steaks. Divide couscous mixture evenly among serving plates with rocket and mint. Top with steak.

ITALIAN-STYLE BEEF AND TOMATO MEATLOAF

INGREDIENTS

- 500g beef mince
- 1 egg, lightly whisked
- 3/4 cup (50g) fresh breadcrumbs (made from day-old bread)
- 1/4 cup (40g) pine nuts, lightly toasted
- 1 brown onion, finely chopped
- 1/3 cup finely chopped basil
- 200g vine-ripened cherry tomatoes, halved
- 200g cup mushrooms, halved or quartered
- 1 cup (250ml) tomato pasta sauce
- 2 garlic cloves, crushed

METHOD

Step 1: Preheat oven to 200°C. Grease a 10cm x 20cm (base measurement) loaf pan. Combine the mince, egg, breadcrumbs, pine nuts, half the onion and half the basil in a bowl. Season. Press mince mixture into prepared pan.

Step 2: Grease a large deep baking tray. Invert mince mixture onto prepared tray. Remove the pan. Lightly spray meatloaf with olive oil spray. Bake for 15 mins.

Step 3: Combine the tomato, mushroom, pasta sauce, garlic, remaining onion and remaining basil in a clean bowl. Season. Spoon tomato mixture over and around the meatloaf. Bake for 30-35 mins or until the meatloaf is cooked through.

BEEF, BROCCOLI AND BLACK BEAN NOODLES

INGREDIENTS

- 200g egg noodles
- 1 tbs sunflower oil
- 500g Coles Australian No Added Hormones Beef Stir-Fry strips
- 1 brown onion, thinly sliced
- 2 garlic cloves, crushed
- 1 head broccoli, cut into florets
- 1/4 cup (60ml) black bean sauce
- 1 bunch choy sum, trimmed
- Sliced red chilli, to serve (optional)
- Coriander leaves, to serve

METHOD

Step 1: Cook the noodles in a saucepan of boiling water following packet directions. Drain, reserving 1/3 cup (80ml) cooking liquid.

Step 2: Meanwhile, heat 2 tsp oil in a wok or large deep frying pan over high heat. Stir-fry the beef, in 2 batches, for 2 mins or until browned. Transfer to a plate.

Step 3: Heat remaining oil in wok or pan over medium-high heat. Add onion, garlic and broccoli. Stir-fry for 4 mins or until broccoli is tender. Return beef to wok or pan with noodles, black bean sauce and reserved cooking liquid. Toss until combined and heated through.

Step 4: Add choy sum to the wok or pan and stir-fry for 1 min or until just wilted. Serve with chilli, if using, and coriander.

SICHUAN BEEF AND BUCKWHEAT STIR-FRY

INGREDIENTS

- 1 cup raw buckwheat, rinsed, drained
- 500g beef rump steak, trimmed, thinly slice
- 2 tsp Sichuan peppercorns, crushed
- 2 tbsp peanut oil
- 1 brown onion, cut into thin wedges
- 1 red capsicum, chopped
- 2 garlic cloves, crushed
- 1cm piece fresh ginger, finely grated
- 125g snow peas, trimmed, halved diagonally
- 2 baby bok choy, trimmed, quartered
- 1/4 cup oyster sauce
- 1 tbsp soy sauce
- 1 tbsp rice wine vinegar
- Sliced red chilli, to serve
- Fresh coriander leaves, to serve

METHOD

Step 1: Cook buckwheat in a medium saucepan of boiling water for 15 to 20 minutes or until tender. Drain. Rinse under cold water. Drain.

Step 2: Meanwhile, combine beef and peppercorns in a bowl. Heat a wok over high heat. Add 2 teaspoons oil. Swirl to coat. Add half the beef. Stir-fry for 2 to 3 minutes or until browned. Transfer to a bowl. Cover to keep warm. Repeat with another 2 teaspoons of remaining oil and remaining beef. Remove wok from heat. Carefully wipe clean.

Step 3: Return wok to heat. Add remaining oil. Swirl to coat. Add onion. Stir-fry for 3 minutes or until golden. Add capsicum, garlic and ginger. Stir-fry for 2 minutes or until fragrant and starting to soften. Add snow peas and bok choy. Stir-fry for 1 minute. Add oyster sauce, soy sauce, vinegar, buckwheat, beef and any resting juices. Stir-fry for 2 to 3 minutes or until heated through. Sprinkle with chilli and coriander leaves. Serve.

BEEF AND MUSHROOM KEBABS WITH BUCKWHEAT SALAD

INGREDIENTS

- 1 tbsp finely chopped fresh rosemary
- 1/4 cup extra virgin olive oil
- 1/3 cup balsamic vinegar
- 3 garlic cloves, crushed
- 450g beef rump steak, trimmed, cut into 2cm pieces
- 250g cup mushrooms, halved
- 1 bunch baby beetroot, trimmed
- 1 cup buckwheat, rinsed
- 1 cup Massel salt reduced chicken style liquid stock
- 1/2 cup orange juice
- 1 cup fresh flat-leaf parsley leaves
- 1/2 small red onion, thinly sliced
- 2 tbsp roughly chopped dry roasted hazelnuts
- 50g reduced-fat fetta, crumbled

METHOD

Step 1: Preheat oven to 200C/180C fan-forced. Combine rosemary, 2 tablespoons oil, 2 tablespoons vinegar and 2/3 garlic in a large glass or ceramic bowl. Stir in beef and mushroom. Refrigerate for 1 hour.

Step 2: Meanwhile, wash beetroot and pat dry. Wrap each in foil. Place on a baking tray. Roast for 40 minutes or until tender. Set aside until cool enough to handle. Wearing disposable gloves, peel beetroot. Cut into wedges. Place beetroot in a bowl. Add 1 tablespoon remaining vinegar and remaining garlic. Season. Toss to coat.

Step 3: Meanwhile, heat a large saucepan over medium-high heat. Add buckwheat. Cook, stirring, for 1 minute. Add stock and juice. Stir to combine. Bring to the boil. Reduce heat to medium. Simmer, covered, for 15 to 20 minutes or until buckwheat is tender and liquid has been absorbed. Remove from heat. Stand for 5 minutes. Fluff mixture with a fork. Transfer to a large bowl.

Step 4: Thread beef and mushroom onto skewers. Heat a barbecue grill on medium-high heat. Cook for 2 minutes each side for medium or until cooked to your liking.

Step 5: Add parsley, onion, hazelnuts and fetta to buckwheat. Season. Toss to combine. Arrange buckwheat salad, beetroot and skewers on a serving platter. Whisk remaining oil and vinegar in a small bowl. Drizzle over buckwheat mixture. Serve.

SRI LANKAN BEEF AND COCONUT CURRY

INGREDIENTS

- 1 1/2 tbsp peanut oil
- 1.2kg beef chuck steak, cut into 3cm pieces
- 1 brown onion, thinly sliced
- 3 garlic cloves, finely chopped
- 1 tbsp finely chopped fresh ginger
- 1 long fresh green chilli, deseeded, thinly sliced
- 1 tbsp curry powder
- 3 tsp ground coriander
- 2 tsp Massel Chicken Stock Powder
- 180ml (3/4 cup) passata
- 350g sweet potato, peeled, cut into 3cm pieces
- 270ml can coconut milk
- 2 tbsp tamarind puree
- 2 fresh curry leaf sprigs, plus extra sprigs, to serve
- 5 cardamom pods, crushed
- 1 cinnamon stick
- 3 tsp brown sugar
- Roti bread, warmed, to serve

- Steamed rice, to serve

METHOD

Step 1: Heat 1 tablespoon oil in a large frying pan over high heat. Cook the beef, in batches, for 5 minutes or until evenly browned. Use tongs to transfer the beef to a slow cooker.

Step 2: Heat the remaining 2 teaspoons oil in the pan. Add the onion. Reduce heat to medium. Cook, stirring often, for 5 minutes or until tender. Add the garlic, ginger and chilli. Cook, stirring, for 1 minute or until aromatic. Add the curry powder and coriander. Stir to coat. Add the stock powder, passata and 250ml (1 cup) water. Stir to combine.

Step 3: Pour the curry mixture into the slow cooker. Add the sweet potato, coconut milk, tamarind, curry leaves, cardamom and cinnamon. Stir to combine. Cover and cook on High for 4 hours or until the beef is very tender.

Step 4: Stir through the sugar and season. Sprinkle with extra curry leaves and serve with roti and rice.

SPEEDY BEEF PAD SEE EW

INGREDIENTS

- 340g pkt Coles Asia Thick Egg Noodles
- 500g Coles Australian No Added Hormones Beef Rump Steak, thinly sliced
- 600g pkt Coles Rainbow Stir-Fry Mix
- 205g pkt pad see ew cooking sauce
- Coriander sprigs, to serve

EQUIPMENT

Wok or large non-stick frying pan

METHOD

Step 1: Cook the noodles in a large saucepan of boiling water for 4 mins or until tender. Drain well.

Step 2: Meanwhile, heat a wok or large non-stick frying pan over high heat. Add half the beef. Stir-fry for 1-2 mins or until just cooked through. Transfer to a plate. Repeat with the remaining beef.

Step 3: Return the beef to the wok or pan with the stir-fry mix, cooking sauce from the pad see ew packet and noodles. Stir-fry for 2-3 mins or until the vegetables are tender and the mixture is heated through. Season.

Step 4: Divide the beef mixture among serving bowls. Season. Sprinkle with chilli flakes from the pad see ew packet and coriander to serve.

POTATO, BEEF AND FETTA
TRAY BAKE

INGREDIENTS

- 4 Red Royale or white potatoes, finely chopped
- 1 tbs olive oil
- 1 tbs Moroccan seasoning
- 1 red onion
- 1 carrot, peeled, finely chopped
- 500g Coles Australian No Added Hormones 4 Star Beef Mince
- 400g can diced tomatoes
- 1 cup (120g) frozen peas
- 100g fetta, crumbled
- 1 cup coriander leaves
- 1/2 cup (140g) Greek-style yoghurt
- 1/4 tsp Moroccan seasoning, extra

METHOD

Step 1: Preheat oven to 220°C. Line a roasting pan with baking paper. Combine the potato, half the oil and half the Moroccan seasoning in a large bowl. Toss to combine. Spread the potato mixture evenly over the base of the prepared pan. Bake for 15 mins or until just tender.

Step 2: Meanwhile, thinly slice half the onion crossways. Transfer to a small bowl. Finely chop the remaining onion.

Step 3: Heat remaining oil in a large frying pan over medium heat. Add the carrot and chopped onion. Cook, stirring, for 3 mins or until the onion softens. Add the mince and cook, stirring with a wooden spoon to break up any lumps, for 5 mins or until the mince changes colour. Add the remaining Moroccan seasoning and stir to combine. Add the tomato. Stir to combine. Bring to a simmer. Cook for 2 mins or until heated through. Add peas and stir to combine.

Step 4: Spoon the mince mixture over the potato in the pan. Sprinkle with fetta. Bake for 10 mins or until heated through.

Step 5: Top mince mixture with coriander, sliced onion and yoghurt. Sprinkle with extra Moroccan seasoning. Season.

PEPPER CRUSTED BEEF TOMAHAWK STEAKS

INGREDIENTS

- 1 tbs coarsely ground black pepper
- 2 tbs olive oil
- 20g butter, melted
- 1 garlic clove, crushed
- 2 tsp chopped thyme
- 2 Coles Australian No Added Hormones Beef Tomahawk Steaks
- 3 Lebanese cucumbers, peeled into ribbons
- 2 peaches, stoned, cut into wedges
- 1/2 small red onion, thinly sliced
- 60g pkt Coles Australian Baby Rocket
- 1/4 cup (60ml) Coles Raspberry Balsamic Salad Dressing

METHOD

Step 1: Combine the pepper, oil, butter, garlic and thyme in a large bowl. Add the steaks and turn to coat.

Step 2 :Heat a covered barbecue on high. Cook the steaks on barbecue grill for 5 mins each side or until golden brown. Place in a disposable baking tray. Roast in covered barbecue using indirect heat for 18-20 mins for medium or until cooked to your liking. Set aside for 5 mins to rest.

Step 3: Meanwhile, combine the cucumber, peach, onion and rocket in a large bowl. Season.

Step 4: Drizzle the salad with the salad dressing. Slice steaks and serve with the salad.

WARM WASABI BEEF AND ZOODLE SALAD

INGREDIENTS

- 1 teaspoon wasabi paste
- 2 tablespoons salt-reduced tamari
- 1 1/2 tablespoons mirin
- 2 x 250g lean beef rump steaks, fat trimmed
- 145g (1 cup) frozen shelled edamame
- 250g packet zucchini noodles
- 100g baby spinach
- 1 small red capsicum, deseeded, thinly sliced
- 1/2 small red onion, cut into thin wedges
- 2 teaspoons sesame seeds, toasted

METHOD

Step 1: Combine wasabi, tamari and mirin in a small bowl. Place half the dressing in a shallow dish and add the beef. Turn to coat. Cover and set aside for 30 minutes to marinate. Reserve the remaining dressing.

Step 2: Preheat a chargrill pan or barbecue grill over high. Lightly spray beef with oil. Cook beef for 2-3 minutes each side for medium-rare. Transfer to a plate. Cover loosely with foil and set aside for 5 minutes to rest before thinly slicing.

Step 3: Meanwhile, steam edamame for 2-3 minutes over a saucepan of simmering water, adding the zucchini in the last minute of cooking. Drain.

Step 4: Combine the zucchini, edamame, spinach, capsicum and onion in a large serving bowl. Top with the beef and drizzle over the reserved dressing. Sprinkle with sesame seeds.

RED CURRY BEEF WITH CAULIFLOWER RICE

INGREDIENTS

- 1 tbs sesame oil
- 3 Coles Australian Free Range Eggs, lightly whisked
- 500g Coles Australian No Added Hormones Beef Rump Steak
- 1/4 cup (75g) red curry paste
- 1 red capsicum, seeded, finely chopped
- 2 garlic cloves, crushed
- 300g pkt Coles Australian Cauliflower Rice
- 1 cup (120g) frozen baby peas, thawed

METHOD

Step 1: Heat half the oil in a frying pan over medium-high heat. Add the egg and swirl to coat the base of the pan. Cook for 2 mins or until almost set. Transfer to a clean work surface. Roll into a log and thinly slice crossways.

Step 2: Cook the beef in the pan for 2 mins each side. Brush the top of the beef with curry paste. Turn and cook for 1 min. Brush the top with more curry paste. Turn and cook for 1 min for medium-rare or until cooked to your liking. Transfer to a plate. Cover with foil.

Step 3:Add the capsicum and garlic to the pan and cook, stirring, for 2 mins or until aromatic. Add the cauliflower rice and peas and cook for 2 mins or until cauliflower starts to soften. Add egg and cook, stirring, for 2 mins or until combined and heated through.

Step 4: Divide the cauliflower rice mixture evenly among serving bowls. Season. Thickly slice the beef. Arrange over the cauliflower rice in the bowls.

BEEF RAVIOLI WITH SPINACH PESTO AND PUMPKIN

INGREDIENTS

- 60g baby spinach
- 30g baby rocket
- 1/2 cup (40g) shaved parmesan
- 1 garlic clove, crushed
- 2/3 cup (160ml) olive oil
- 1/2 cup (50g) walnuts, toasted, chopped
- 800g butternut pumpkin, peeled, seeded, thinly sliced lengthways
- 2 zucchini, peeled into ribbons
- 625g pkt Latina Fresh Classic Beef Ravioli
- Baby spinach leaves, extra, to serve
- Baby rocket leaves, extra, to serve
- Shaved parmesan, extra, to serve

METHOD

Step 1 : Process the spinach, rocket, parmesan, garlic, oil and half the walnut in a food processor until almost smooth. Season. Transfer to a bowl. Cover with plastic wrap, pressing directly onto the surface.

Step 2: Heat a barbecue grill or chargrill on medium-high. Spray the pumpkin and zucchini with olive oil spray. Cook pumpkin, in batches, for 2 mins each side or until browned and tender. Transfer to a bowl. Cook zucchini, in batches, for 30 secs each side or until browned and tender. Add to the pumpkin in the bowl.

Step 3:Cook ravioli in a saucepan of boiling water for 5 mins or until ravioli float to the surface and are tender. Drain well.

Step 4: Add ravioli and half the pesto to the pumpkin mixture and toss to combine. Season. Divide among serving plates. Top with remaining walnut, extra spinach, extra rocket and extra parmesan. Drizzle with the remaining pesto to serve.

SPRING BEEF CASSEROLE

INGREDIENTS

- 500g beef chuck steak, cut into 3cm pieces
- 2 tsp smoked paprika
- 2 tbs olive oil
- 1 brown onion, coarsely chopped
- 1 red capsicum, seeded, coarsely chopped
- 2 zucchini, coarsely chopped
- 2 garlic cloves, finely chopped
- 400g pineapple, peeled, chopped
- 1 cup (250ml) Massel Beef Style Liquid Stock
- 2 rosemary sprigs
- 1 cup (200g) couscous
- 1 cup (250ml) boiling water

METHOD

Step 1: Place the beef in a large bowl. Sprinkle with paprika and toss to coat. Heat the oil in a large frying pan over medium heat. Cook the beef, in batches, turning, for 5 mins or until brown all over. Transfer to a slow cooker with the onion, capsicum, zucchini, garlic, pineapple, stock and rosemary. Season. Cover and cook for 6 hours on low or until the beef is tender. Remove the rosemary and discard.

Step 2: Place the couscous in a large heatproof bowl. Pour over the boiling water. Cover with plastic wrap and set aside for 4-5 mins or until the liquid is absorbed. Use a fork to separate the grains.

Step 3: Divide the couscous evenly among serving bowls. Top with the beef mixture. Season to serve.

RECIPE NOTES

Allow for 5 minutes standing time.

SERVE WITH... chopped flat-leaf parsley and chopped basil or basil leaves

Add more veg: Got carrots or potatoes on hand? Chop and add them to this tasty stew.

SNACKS RECIPES

CHEESY KETO SNACKS

INGREDIENTS

- 155g (1 1/2 cups) Perfect Bakes 3 cheese blend
- 80g (2/3 cup) almond meal
- 60g cream cheese
- 1 egg
- 1 teaspoon finely chopped fresh rosemary leaves
- 1 tablespoon sunflower seeds
- 2 teaspoons linseeds
- Smashed avocado, to serve

METHOD

Step 1: Preheat oven to 180C/160C fan forced. Line 2 baking trays with baking paper, with an extra sheet for rolling. Place the cheese, almond meal, cream cheese and 60ml (1/4 cup) water in a medium saucepan. Cook, stirring with a wooden spoon, over medium heat for 3 minutes or until melted and combined. Remove from heat.

Step 2: Working quickly, add the egg and rosemary and beat well until the egg is absorbed. Place half of the mixture on 1 prepared tray. Scatter with half of the sunflower seeds and linseeds. Cover with the extra sheet of paper and use a rolling pin to roll to a thin 2-3mm-thick rectangle.

Step 3: Remove the top sheet. Use a pizza cutter to cut into wedges. Repeat with the remaining mixture and seeds.

Step 4: Bake for 12 minutes or until golden. Set aside to cool. Serve with avocado if desired. Snacks will store for up to two days at room temperature in an airtight container.

AUSSIE SNACKS CHRISTMAS HOUSE

INGREDIENTS

- 250g cream cheese, at room temperature
- 1/2 x 40g packet French onion soup mix
- 2 x 125g packets sesame and sea salt grissini breadsticks
- 5-6 twiggy sticks
- 8 thin slices pepperoni
- Small rectangle piece tasty cheese
- 8 pimento-stuffed green olives
- 1 Cheds biscuit, halved
- 5 mini Chicken Crimpy biscuits
- 2 Burger Rings
- Fresh rosemary sprigs
- Finely grated parmesan cheese, to dust

METHOD

Step 1: Place the cream cheese and soup mix in a medium bowl. Use a wooden spoon to beat until smooth and creamy. Spoon into a piping bag. Use scissors to snip off a small piece at the tip of the bag.

Step 2: Cut 10 grissini sticks into 12cm lengths and 10 sticks into 10cm lengths. Pipe some of the cream cheese mixture on a board and top with 1 x 12cm grissini stick. Continue layering with 4 more sticks to form one side of the house. Repeat process with 10cm sticks to build the back of the house. Pipe cream cheese on some of the remaining bread sticks and press on the inside of the house as support while building. Repeat process to build the remaining side and front of the house.

Step 3: Using the picture as a guide, trim the remaining breadsticks into 4 smaller pieces, graduating in size to form a gable at the front and back of the house. Secure in place with cream cheese mixture.

Step 4: Place a long breadstick across the full length of the top of the house. Using the picture as a guide, alternate halved twiggy sticks and breadsticks to form the roof, securing with cream cheese mixture.

Step 5: Cut the pepperoni in half and secure to the top of the roof. Thinly slice four olives. Pipe a line of cream cheese on top of pepperoni and decorate with some of the olives. Trim the base of the tasty cheese rectangle at an angle for the chimney and secure on roof. Using cream cheese mixture, secure Cheds biscuit to front of house to form a door and 2 Chicken Crimpy biscuits to side of house to form windows. Using picture as guide, secure Burger Rings and sliced olives to front of house to form windows.

Step 6: Halve remaining olives. Place 4 small sprigs of rosemary in halved olives to make 'trees' and place at the side of the house. Make 'wood piles' with a twiggy stick cut into thin pieces. Form a small sprig of rosemary into a wreath and secure over the doorway. Using cream cheese mixture, pipe on a door knob and 'smoke' on the chimney. Use any remaining cream cheese mixture to fill gaps and pipe on 'icicles'.

Step 7: Top with finely grated parmesan and secure thee remaining Chicken Crimpy biscuits as stepping stones.

RECIPE NOTES

Make close to serving time as biscuits will start to soften. Serve with extra dip on the side if desired.

KETO SNACK BARS

INGREDIENTS

- 85g (1/2 cup) almonds
- 55g (1/2 cup) walnut halves
- 80g (1/2 cup) macadamia nuts
- 80g (1/2 cup) pepitas
- 85g (1 cup) desiccated coconut
- 1 tsp ground cinnamon
- 130g (1/2 cup) peanut coconut spread
- 60g (1/4 cup) solidified coconut oil
- 2 tsp vanilla bean paste

METHOD

Step 1: Lightly grease and line a 16 x 26cm (base measurement) lamington pan with baking paper.

Step 2: Process the almonds, walnuts, macadamia nuts and pepitas in a food processor until coarsely chopped. Transfer to a large bowl. Stir in the coconut and cinnamon.

Step 3: Combine the peanut spread, coconut oil and vanilla in a small saucepan and cook, stirring, over low heat for 3-5 minutes or until melted and well combined.

Step 4: Add the peanut mixture to the dry ingredients and mix until well combined. Press mixture firmly into prepared pan, smoothing surface with the back of a spoon. Cover and place in the fridge for 2-3 hours or until firm. Cut into 16 bars.

RECIPE NOTES

These bars need to be kept refrigerated. They can also be kept in an airtight container in the freezer.

WATERMELON AND YOGHURT POPS

INGREDIENTS

- 1/4 watermelon
- Vanilla yoghurt, to serve
- Fruit (such as pomegranate seeds and chopped mango, peach, blueberry, raspberry, kiwifruit and strawberry), to serve

METHOD

Step 1: Line a baking tray with baking paper. Cut the watermelon into wedges. Insert iceblock sticks. Place on the lined tray. Freeze for 1 hour.

Step 2: Spoon yoghurt over the watermelon on the tray. Sprinkle with fruit. Freeze until firm.

HOMMUS, CHEESE AND CARROT SNACK BOX

INGREDIENTS

- 400g can chickpeas, drained, rinsed
- 2 cloves garlic, crushed
- 100ml olive oil
- 1 tbsp tahini paste
- 1/2 tsp ground cumin
- 1 lemon, juiced
- Turkish bread, toasted and cut into fingers to serve
- Cheese, cut into thin batons, to serve
- 1 celery stick, cut into thin batons, to serve
- 1 carrot, cut into thin batons, to serve

METHOD

Step 1: Place chickpeas, garlic, oil, lemon juice, tahini paste and cumin in a food processor and process until combined. Add 1/4 cup of water and process again until smooth.

Step 2: Place hommus in a container and serve with toasted Turkish bread, cheese, celery and carrot sticks.

CHIA, ALMOND AND CACAO BALLS

INGREDIENTS

- 1 vanilla bean, split
- 2 tbsp white chia seeds (see box)
- 2 tbsp unsweetened almond milk
- 1 cup blanched almonds
- 1 cup walnuts
- 1/2 cup shredded coconut
- 1/3 cup cacao powder (see Notes)
- 1/4 tsp sea salt
- 1/2 tsp ground cinnamon
- 1/2 cup almond spread
- 2 tbsp rice malt syrup

EQUIPMENT

Food processor.

METHOD

Step 1: Scrape seeds from vanilla bean. Discard vanilla pod. Place chia seeds and milk in a small bowl. Stir to combine.

Step 2: Meanwhile, process almonds, walnuts and 1/4 cup coconut until finely chopped. Transfer to a large bowl. Add cacao, salt, cinnamon and vanilla seeds. Stir to combine. Add almond spread, rice malt syrup and chia mixture. Stir to combine, adding an extra 2 teaspoons of rice malt syrup to bind mixture, if needed.

Step 3: Place remaining coconut in a shallow dish. Using 1 tablespoon of mixture, press and roll mixture together to form a ball. Roll ball in coconut to lightly coat. Place on a large baking tray lined with baking paper. Repeat with remaining mixture and coconut. Store in an airtight container in the fridge for up to 1 week. Remove from fridge 10 minutes before serving.

NUTS AND BOLTS SLICE

INGREDIENTS

- 100g pitted fresh dates, chopped
- 150g (1 cup) salted peanuts
- 80g (1/2 cup) natural almonds, chopped
- 45g (1/4 cup) pepitas
- 35g puffed rice
- 2 tbsp honey
- 2 tbsp almond butter
- 2 tbsp macadamia oil
- 1 tsp ground cinnamon

METHOD

Step 1: Preheat oven to 160/140C fan-forced. Lightly spray a 20 x 30cm baking pan with oil and line the base and 2 long sides with baking paper.

Step 2: Place the dates and 2 tablespoons boiling water in a small bowl. Set aside for 3 minutes to soak. Use a fork to coarsely mash.

Step 3: Meanwhile, process the peanuts, almonds and pepitas in a food processor until coarsely chopped. Transfer to a large bowl. Add the puffed rice and stir to combine.

Step 4: Place the date mixture, honey, almond butter, oil and cinnamon in a small saucepan. Cook, stirring, for 2 minutes or until well combined and warmed through. Add to the nut mixture and stir until well combined.

Step 5: Press the mixture firmly into the prepared pan, smoothing the surface with the back of a spoon. Bake for 35-40 minutes or until a deep golden brown. Set aside to cool completely in the pan.

Step 6: Cut the slice into 20 pieces. Store in an airtight container for up to 5 days.

'FERRERO ROCHER' BALLS

INGREDIENTS

- 100g pitted fresh dates
- 140g roasted hazelnuts, skins removed
- 75g digestive biscuits
- 3 teaspoons raw cacao powder
- 1/2 teaspoon vanilla extract
- 150g dark (78%) chocolate, melted, cooled slightly

METHOD

Step 1: Place the dates in a heatproof bowl. Cover with boiling water. Set aside for 10 minutes. Drain.

Step 2: Place 60g of the hazelnuts, biscuits and cacao in a food processor. Process until coarsely chopped. Add dates and vanilla. Process until almost smooth but mixture still has a little texture.

Step 3: Line a baking tray with baking paper. Roll 2 teaspoonfuls of mixture at a time into balls. Press a whole hazelnut into the centre of each and re-roll to enclose.

Step 4: Coarsely chop the remaining hazelnuts. Place melted chocolate in a bowl. Use a fork to dip the balls in the chocolate to coat. Transfer to prepared tray, draining off excess chocolate. Sprinkle with chopped hazelnuts. Place in the fridge until set or ready to serve.

CHOCOLATE COOKIES

INGREDIENTS

- 10 dates, pitted, finely chopped
- 60ml (1/4 cup) boiling water
- 90g (1 cup) rolled oats
- 400g can Coles Chickpeas, drained, rinsed
- 45g (1/2 cup) desiccated coconut
- 75g (1/3 cup) solidified coconut oil, melted, cooled
- 2 tbsp cocoa powder, plus extra to flatten
- 1 tsp baking powder
- 1 egg
- 1 tsp vanilla extract

METHOD

Step 1: Preheat oven to 180C /160C fan forced and line 2 baking trays with baking paper. Place the dates in a heatproof bowl and cover with water. Set aside for 2 minutes to soften. Use a fork to coarsely mash

Step 2: Process the oats in a food processor and until chopped. Add the dates, chickpeas, coconut, coconut oil, cocoa powder, baking powder, egg and vanilla. Process to combine. Transfer to a bowl and set aside for 30 minutes to allow to thicken.

Step 3: Roll level tablespoons of the mixture into balls and place on the prepared trays. Dip the tines of a fork in cocoa to prevent sticking, and press into each cookie first one way and then the other (biscuits should be 1cm thick). Keep dipping the fork into cocoa as needed.

Step 4: Bake cookies for 12 minutes. Cool on the tray for 5 minutes, then transfer to a wire rack to cool completely. Store in an airtight container for up to 4 days, (biscuits will become softer).

BANANA SOFT SERVE

INGREDIENTS

- 6 bananas, peeled, chopped and frozen
- 60ml (1/4 cup) lemon juice

METHOD

Step 1: Process frozen banana and lemon juice in a food processor, scraping down sides frequently, until mixture is smooth and resembles soft serve ice-cream. Transfer to a metal loaf pan. Place in the freezer for 2 hours or until just firm but still scoop-able.

SUGAR-FREE MANGO AND COCONUT BALLS

INGREDIENTS

- 125g dried mango
- 50g (2/3 cup) shredded coconut
- 50g (1/2 cup) rolled oats
- 145g (1 cup) raw cashews
- 60g (3/4 cup) desiccated coconut
- 1 tbsp finely grated lime zest
- 1 tsp vanilla extract

METHOD

Step 1: Use kitchen scissors to cut the mango into small (about 1.5cm) pieces. Place in a heatproof bowl and pour 125 ml (½ cup) of boiling water. Set aside for 10-15 minutes, stirring occasionally, or until mango has softened and water absorbed.

Step 2: Place the shredded coconut in a frying pan and stir over medium heat for about 3 minutes or until golden. Transfer to a plate to cool.

Step 3: Process the oats a food processor until well chopped. Add the cashews, desiccated coconut, lime zest, vanilla, a pinch of salt and mango (with any water that may not have absorbed). Process until well combined.

Step 4: Roll level tablespoons of the mixture into balls. Roll in toasted coconut to lightly coat. Store in an airtight container for up to 1 week.

SPICY AND SWEET ROASTED NUTS

Preparation time: 5 minutes

Cooking time: 15 minutes

Servings: 4

Ingredients:

- 1-pound (454g) walnut halves and pieces
- ½ cup granulated sugar
- 3 tablespoons vegetable oil
- 1 teaspoon cayenne pepper
- ½ teaspoon fine salt

Directions

- Soak the walnuts in a large bowl with boiling water for a minute or two. Drain the walnuts.

- Stir in the sugar, oil, and cayenne pepper to coat well. Spread the walnuts in a single layer in the baking pan.
- Select "Roast" set temperature to 325 degrees Fahrenheit (163 degrees Celsius) and set time to 15 minutes.
- After 7 or 8 minutes, remove, and stir the nuts. Return, and check frequently.
- When done, the walnuts should be dark golden brown. Sprinkle the nuts with the salt and let cool. Serve warm.

Nutrition:

- Calories 205
- Carbohydrates 5g
- Fat 20g
- Protein 4g

COCONUT AND STRAWBERRY MUFFINS

INGREDIENTS

- 35g (1/4 cup) coconut flour
- 190g (1 1/4 cups) self-raising flour
- 185ml (3/4 cup) buttermilk
- 60ml (1/4 cup) liquid coconut oil
- 3 eggs, lightly whisked
- 120g tub apple puree
- 1 tsp vanilla extract
- 250g strawberries, washed, hulled, quartered (or chopped if using large strawberries)
- 10g (1/4 cup) flaked coconut

METHOD

Step 1: Preheat oven to 180C/160C fan forced. Line twelve 80ml (1/3 cup) muffin pans with paper cases. Sift flours into a large bowl and make a well in the centre. Whisk the buttermilk, oil, egg, apple puree and vanilla in a large jug.

Step 2: Add the buttermilk mixture to the flour mixture and stir until just combined. Gently fold in half the strawberry. Divide the mixture among the prepared pans. Sprinkle with remaining strawberry and coconut.

Step 3: Bake for 20-25 minutes or until golden brown and a skewer inserted into the centre comes out clean. Transfer to a wire rack to cool.

PEANUT BUTTER AND JAM SLICE WITH VANILLA SALT

INGREDIENTS

- 235g (1 1/2 cups) spelt flour
- 1 1/2 teaspoons baking powder
- 85g (1/2 cup) coconut sugar, plus 2 teaspoons extra
- 140g (1 1/2 cup) peanut butter with hemp seeds
- 35g (1/4 cup) coconut butter
- 1 teaspoon vanilla extract
- 2 eggs
- 90g (1/4 cup) raspberry sugar-free jam or fruit spread, plus extra to serve (optional)
- 80g (1/2 cup) roasted unsalted peanuts, coarsely chopped
- 1 vanilla bean, split, seeds scraped
- 1 teaspoon pink Himalayan salt flakes
- Fresh raspberries, to serve (optional)

METHOD

Step 1: Preheat oven to 180C/160C fan forced. Line a 20 x 30cm slice pan with baking paper, allowing the long sides to overhang.

Step 2: Place flour, baking powder, sugar, peanut butter, coconut butter and vanilla extract in a food processor.Process until coarse crumbs form. Add eggs and process until mixture just starts to come together.

Step 3: Use slightly damp hands to press mixture into base of prepared pan and smooth the surface. Use the end of a wooden spoon, dipped in flour to prevent sticking, to make at least 60 indents all over the base. Spoon the jam into a sealable plastic bag and snip off the corner. Pipe jam into indents. Sprinkle with the chopped peanuts.

Step 4: Mix the vanilla bean seeds, salt and extra 2 teaspoons sugar in a small bowl. Gently rub with your fingertips until combined. Sprinkle over slice. Bake for 25-30 minutes or until light golden. Set aside, still in the pan, to cool completely. Remove from pan and cut into 20 pieces. Top with the extra jam and fresh raspberries, if you like.

'CHERRY RIPE' BLISS BALLS

INGREDIENTS

- 100g dried cherries
- 100g (about 6) pitted dates, chopped
- 45g (1/2 cup) desiccated coconut, plus 2-3 tbs, extra
- 2 tbs cacao powder, plus 2-3 tbs, extra
- 1 tablespoon coconut oil
- 1 tablespoon honey

METHOD

Step 1: Place all the ingredients in a food processor and process until well combined. Roll tablespoonfuls of the mixture into balls. Roll in extra coconut or cacao to coat.

BANANA BREAD

INGREDIENTS

- 100g (1 cup) coconut flour
- 160g (1 1/4 cups) wholemeal spelt flour
- 3 1/2 teaspoons baking powder
- 40g (1/2 cup) desiccated coconut
- 1 teaspoon ground cinnamon
- 50g (1/3 cup) coconut or rapadura sugar
- 3 large bananas, mashed (310g flesh), plus 1 extra, for decoration
- 3 eggs
- 80ml (1/3 cup) olive oil
- 160ml (2/3 cup) oat, soy or rice milk
- Maple syrup, to serve (optional)

METHOD

Step 1: Preheat oven to 180C/ 160C fan forced. Grease and line a

7.5cm deep, 22.5 x 8.5cm (base measurement) loaf pan with non-stick baking paper, allowing the long sides to overhang.

Step 2: Combine the flours, baking powder, coconut, cinnamon and sugar in a large bowl. Make a well in the centre. Add the banana, eggs, oil and milk and stir to combine. Pour the mixture into the prepared pan. Smooth surface. Very finely slice the remaining banana. Place banana slices, overlapping each over, to cover the entire surface of the loaf.

Step 3: Bake for 45-55 minutes or until a skewer comes out clean when inserted in the centre. Slice and serve with a drizzle of maple syrup if desired.

MARSHMALLOW BUBBLE BARS

INGREDIENTS

- 5 cups Rice Bubbles
- 2 cups (200g) vanilla marshmallows (see notes)
- 100g butter, chopped
- 50g CADBURY Baking White Chocolate, melted
- 2 tablespoons rainbow choc chips

EQUIPMENT

16cm x 26cm (base) slice pan

METHOD

Step 1: Grease a 16cm x 26cm (base) slice pan. Line with baking paper, extending paper 2cm above edges on all sides.

Step 2: Place Rice Bubbles in a large bowl. Place marshmallows and butter in a large microwave-safe bowl. Microwave on HIGH (100%)

for 1 minute, stirring every 30 seconds or until mixture is smooth. Add to Rice Bubbles. Stir to coat well.

Step 3: Press mixture firmly and evenly into prepared pan. Drizzle with white chocolate. Sprinkle with rainbow choc chips. Refrigerate for 2 hours or until set.

Step 4: Cut into 20 bars. Wrap each bar in plastic wrap. Refrigerate until required.

RECIPE NOTES

You will need a 400g packet of marshmallows. Only use the white ones.

We used the Queen brand of rainbow choc chips.

CHEESE STRAWS

INGREDIENTS

- 1 1/3 cups plain flour, sifted
- 1/2 tsp salt
- 1/4 tsp cayenne pepper
- 125g butter, chilled, chopped
- 250g aged cheddar, grated (see notes)
- 1 egg, lightly beaten
- 1 tbsp lemon juice

METHOD

Step 1: Preheat oven to 180C/160C fan-forced. Line 3 large baking trays with baking paper.

Step 2: Combine flour, salt and cayenne pepper in a bowl. Rub in butter until mixture resembles breadcrumbs. Add cheese, egg and lemon juice, mixing with your hands to form a dough (add extra lemon juice, if needed).

Step 3: Place 1/2 the dough on a well-floured surface. Roll out to form a 3mm-thick, 20cm x 40cm rectangle. Trim edges to make straight. Cut crossways into 5mm strips (see notes). Repeat with remaining dough. Place strips on prepared trays.

Step 4: Bake, 1 tray at a time, for 10 to 12 minutes or until ends just start to turn golden (see notes). Cool on trays. Serve.

SALTY BAKED ALMONDS

Preparation time: 5 minutes

Cooking time: 25 minutes

Servings: 4

Ingredients:

- 1 cup of raw almonds
- 1 egg white, beaten
- ½ teaspoon coarse sea salt

Directions

- Spread the almonds in the baking pan in an even layer.
- Choose the "Convection Bake" set temperature to 350 degrees Fahrenheit (180 degrees Celsius) and set time to 20 minutes.
- Remove, then coat the almonds with the egg white and

sprinkle with the salt. Return the pan to the oven within 5 minutes.

- Cool completely before serving.

Nutrition:

- Calories 180
- Carbohydrates 5g
- Fat 16g
- Protein: 6g

ZUCCHINI AND FETA MUFFINS

INGREDIENTS

- 2 tbsp extra virgin olive oil
- 3 green shallots, trimmed, thinly sliced
- 1 garlic clove, crushed
- 1 tsp finely grated lemon rind
- 2 zucchini, trimmed
- 320g (2 cups) wholemeal self-raising flour
- Pinch of cayenne pepper
- 375ml (1 1/2 cups) buttermilk
- 125g (1/2 cup) low-fat fresh ricotta
- 2 eggs
- 125g reduced-fat feta, crumbled

METHOD

Step 1: Preheat the oven to 190C/170C fan forced. Lightly grease twelve 80ml (1/3 cup) muffin pans.

Step 2: Combine the oil, shallot and garlic in a small frying pan. Heat gently over low heat until the oil just starts to bubble and the shallot has softened slightly. Transfer to a bowl (with all the oil). Stir in the lemon rind and set aside to cool.

Step 3: Use a julienne peeler to cut the zucchini into long thin strips (or coarsely grate).

Step 4: Place the flour in a large bowl, add the cayenne pepper and season with salt. Make a well in the centre. Whisk the buttermilk, ricotta and eggs together in a jug until smooth. Pour the milk mixture and shallot mixture into the well and stir until just combined. Fold in nearly all the zucchini and feta, reserving a little of both to decorate the tops of the muffins.

Step 5: Divide the mixture among the prepared pans (they will be very full) and top with the reserved zucchini and feta. Bake for 30-35 minutes or until the muffins spring back when gently touched. Set aside for 5 minutes to cool slightly. Use a flat-bladed knife to gently loosen each muffin and remove from the pan. Eat warm or at room temperature.

PAPPA'S ANZAC BISCUITS

INGREDIENTS

- 150g (1 cup) plain flour
- 90g (1 cup) rolled oats
- 85g (1 cup) desiccated coconut
- 100g (1/2 cup, firmly packed) brown sugar
- 55g (1/4 cup) caster sugar
- 125g butter, chopped
- 2 tbsp golden syrup
- 1/2 tsp bicarbonate of soda

METHOD

Step 1: Preheat the oven to 160C/140C fan forced. Line 2 baking trays with baking paper.

Step 2: Combine the flour, rolled oats, coconut and combined sugars in a large bowl.

Step 3: Stir the butter, golden syrup and 2 tbs water in a small saucepan over medium heat until the butter melts and the mixture is smooth. Stir in the bicarb. Add to the flour mixture and stir until well combined.

Step 4: Roll level tablespoonfuls of the dough into balls and place, about 5cm apart, on the prepared trays. Flatten until about 1cm thick. Bake, swapping trays halfway through cooking, for 15-20 minutes or until golden. Set aside for 10 minutes to cool slightly on the tray before transferring to wire racks to cool completely.

CHICKEN AND VEGETABLE SAUSAGE ROLLS

INGREDIENTS

- 1 cup (70g) fresh wholemeal breadcrumbs
- 500g Lilydale Free Range Chicken Mince
- 1 egg, plus 1 extra lightly beaten egg
- 1 zucchini, finely grated
- 1 carrot, finely grated
- 1/2 onion, grated
- 1/4 cup chopped coriander leaves
- 1/4 cup chopped flat-leaf parsley leaves
- 4 sheets frozen puff pastry, just thawed
- 1 tablespoon sesame seeds
- Tomato or sweet chilli or sauce, optional, to serve

METHOD

Step 1: Preheat the oven to 200°C and line 2 baking sheets with baking paper.

Step 2: Process breadcrumbs, chicken and unbeaten egg in a food processor until well combined. Place in a bowl, mix well with vegetables and herbs, then season.

Step 3: Place 1 pastry sheet on a floured surface and halve. Spoon an eighth of the mixture lengthways along centre of each piece. Fold 1 edge of pastry over and tuck in beside filling, then fold over other side to make a roll, pressing down lightly to seal. Repeat with remaining pastry and filling. Cut rolls into 3cm pieces and cut two small incisions into each roll to prevent splitting. Place on baking sheets, cover and chill for 30 minutes. Brush with beaten egg and sprinkle with sesame seeds. Bake for 25-30 minutes until the rolls are lightly browned and cooked through. Serve with sauce on the side.

CURRIED SWEET POTATO FRIES

Preparation time: 5 minutes

Cooking time: 12 minutes

Servings: 4

Ingredients:

- ½ cup sour cream
- ½ cup mango chutney
- 3 teaspoons curry powder, divided
- 4 cups frozen sweet potato fries
- 1 tablespoon olive oil
- A pinch of salt
- Freshly ground black pepper

Directions

- In a bowl, add together sour cream, chutney, and 1½ teaspoon curry powder. Mix well and let stand.
- Place the sweet potatoes in a sizeable bowl. Pour over the olive oil and sprinkle with the remaining 1½ teaspoon curry powder, salt, and pepper.
- Put the potatoes in the fryer basket. Cook 8 to 12 minutes or until crisp, hot and golden, shaking the basket once during cooking.
- Place the potatoes in a basket and serve with the teaspoon.

Nutrition:

- Calories 323
- Total Fat 10g
- Saturated Fat 4g
- Cholesterol 13mg
- Sodium 138mg
- Carbohydrates 58g
- Fiber 7g
- Protein 3g

HAM AND AVOCADO SANDWICH

INGREDIENTS

- 1/2 avocado, stoned, peeled
- 2 tsp lemon juice
- 1/2 spring onion, chopped
- 2 slices white or wholemeal bread
- 50g ham off the bone

METHOD

Step 1: Mash avocado in a bowl with lemon juice and spring onion.

Step 2: Top 1 slice of bread with avocado mixture and ham. Top with remaining bread. Cut off crusts and discard. Cut the sandwich into fingers.

RASPBERRY MUFFINS

INGREDIENTS

- 1 1/2 cups wholemeal self-raising flour
- 1 cup self-raising flour
- 200g Bulla Cottage Cheese Original
- 1/2 cup honey, melted
- 1/3 cup liquid coconut oil
- 2 eggs, lightly beaten
- 2 teaspoons vanilla extract
- 1 1/3 cups frozen raspberries

METHOD

Step 1: Preheat oven to 190C/170C fan-forced. Line a 12-hole, 1/3-cup-capacity muffin pan with paper cases.

Step 2: Combine flours in a large bowl. Make a well. Add cottage cheese, honey, oil, eggs and vanilla. Mix until just combined (batter will be quite thick at this stage). Fold in raspberries. Divide mixture evenly among paper cases.

Step 3: Bake for 20 to 22 minutes or until golden and just firm to touch. Stand in pan for 5 minutes. Transfer to a wire rack to cool. Serve warm or cold.

LOW-SUGAR LUNCH BOX FRUITY JELLY BITES

INGREDIENTS

- 400g strawberries, hulled, at room temperature
- 2 tsp maple syrup
- 2 tsp vanilla extract
- 2 large mangoes, flesh chopped, at room temperature
- 4 tbsp gelatine powder

METHOD

Step 1: Puree the strawberries in a food processor until smooth. Press through a fine sieve to remove the seeds (you will need 1 cup puree). Discard seeds. Transfer the puree to a bowl. Stir in the maple syrup and 1 teaspoon vanilla. Wash and dry the food processor.

Step 2: Puree the mango and the remaining 1 teaspoon vanilla in the food processor until smooth.

Step 3: Pour 160ml (2/3 cup) water into a microwave-safe cereal bowl (this will provide a good surface area for the gelatine to absorb). Gradually sprinkle 2 tablespoons gelatine evenly over the surface, allowing each addition to absorb water before adding more. If the gelatine isn't taking in the water towards the end, drizzle with 1 tablespoon water. Don't stir the mixture at this stage, as lumps will form. Microwave on High for 30 seconds, then whisk with a fork to dissolve the gelatine. Set aside to cool to room temperature.

Step 4: Use a balloon whisk to stir (not whisk) the gelatine mixture into the strawberry puree. Transfer to a jug. Pour into a 20 x 28cm (base measurement) plastic container. Place in the fridge.

Step 5: Repeat Steps 3 and 4 with the remaining gelatine powder, 160ml (2/3 cup) water and the mango puree. Pour slowly over the strawberry puree. Place in the fridge for 2 hours or until set. Run a flat-bladed knife around the edge of the jelly to loosen from the container. Carefully transfer jelly to a clean work surface. Use assorted 3cm cutters to cut out different shapes or cut jelly into 3cm squares. Store in an airtight container in the fridge for up to 5 days.

CARAMEL POPCORN

INGREDIENTS

- Melted butter, to grease
- 2 tbsp vegetable oil
- 115g (1/2 cup) popping corn
- 215g (1 cup) caster sugar
- 100g butter
- 60ml (1/4 cup) golden syrup
- 60ml (1/4 cup) pouring cream

METHOD

Step 1: Brush a 20 x 30cm slab pan with melted butter. Line the base and 2 long sides with non-stick baking paper, allowing the sides to overhang.

Step 2: Heat the oil in a large heavy-based saucepan with a tight-fitting lid over medium heat. Add the popping corn. Cover and gently shake the pan. When the corn starts to pop, hold the lid and shake the pan occasionally for about 3-4 minutes, or until all the corn has popped. Uncover and set aside to cool.

Step 3: Stir the sugar, butter, golden syrup and cream in a medium saucepan over low heat until the butter melts and the sugar dissolves. Bring the mixture to the boil. Reduce heat to low. Simmer, without stirring, brushing down the side of the pan occasionally with a pastry brush dipped in water, for 10 minutes. Set aside until the bubbles subside.

Step 4: Pour the caramel over the popcorn. Use a large metal spoon to toss until the popcorn is coated completely. Spread the popcorn mixture over the base of the prepared pan and set aside until set. Break into shards.

SUPER-COOL BENTO BOX

INGREDIENTS

- Brown rice crackers, to serve
- Strawberries, to serve

PEA HUMMUS

- 1 cup frozen peas
- 1/2 x 400g can chickpeas, drained, rinsed
- 1 tablespoon tahini
- 2 tablespoons lemon juice
- 1 tablespoon extra virgin olive oil
- 2 teaspoons fresh flat-leaf parsley leaves, finely chopped

MINI SKEWERS

- 1 Lebanese cucumber
- 3 grape tomatoes, halved
- 30g piece gouda cheese, cut into small triangles

HAM, CHEESE AND CARROT WRAPS

- 2 sun-dried tomato and basil wraps
- 30g spreadable cream cheese
- 60g shaved ham
- 1 small carrot, grated

EQUIPMENT

6 toothpicks

METHOD

Step 1: Make Pea hummus: Cook peas following packet directions. Reserve 1 tablespoon. Place remaining peas in a food processor with chickpeas, tahini, lemon juice and oil. Process until smooth. Stir in parsley. Transfer to 2 small airtight containers (see note). Top each with reserved peas.

Step 2: Make Mini skewers: Using a vegetable peeler, peel cucumber into ribbons. Roll up each ribbon. Thread 1 cucumber ribbon, 1/2 tomato and 1 triangle of cheese on 1 toothpick. Repeat with remaining ingredients and toothpicks.

Step 3: Make Ham, cheese and carrot wraps: Place wraps on a flat surface. Spread all over with cream cheese. Top evenly with ham and grated carrot. Roll up to enclose. Cut each wrap into thirds.

Step 4: Pack hummus, skewers, wraps, crackers and strawberries into 2 lunchboxes. Refrigerate until required.

MINI HOT DOGS

INGREDIENTS

- 4 White bread Rolls
- 4 cocktail frankfurts
- tomato sauce, to serve
- 25g (1/4 cup) grated cheddar

METHOD

Step 1: Warm bread rolls. Meanwhile, place frankfurts in a microwave-safe bowl and cover with cold water. Cook on high/800watts/100% for 3 minutes or until heated through. Make a lengthways cut in the top of each roll (don't cut all the way through). Place the frankfurts in the rolls. Drizzle over tomato sauce. Sprinkle with grated cheddar to serve.

VEG LUNCHBOX MUFFINS

INGREDIENTS

- 450g butternut pumpkin, peeled, seeded, roughly chopped
- 2 cups self-raising flour
- 1 small zucchini, coarsely grated
- 1 small carrot, peeled, coarsely grated
- 2 tablespoons chopped fresh chives
- 1/3 cup dry roasted cashews, chopped
- 11/2 cups grated tasty cheese
- 125g Flora Original spread, melted
- 2/3 cup milk
- 2 eggs
- 1/4 cup seed mix

METHOD

Step 1: Place pumpkin on a microwave-safe plate. Drizzle with 1 tablespoon water. Cover with plastic wrap. Microwave on HIGH

(100%) for 5 to 6 minutes or until tender. Drain. Transfer to a bowl. Using a fork, roughly mash pumpkin (you'll need 1 cup). Set aside to cool.

Step 2: Preheat oven to 180C/160C fan-forced. Grease a 12-hole (1/3-cup capacity) muffin pan.

Step 3: Place flour, zucchini, carrot, chives, cashews and 1 1/4 cups cheese in a large bowl. Stir until well combined. Season with salt and pepper. Make a well. Whisk spread, milk, eggs and pumpkin together. Add to flour mixture. Stir until mixture is just combined.

Step 4: Divide mixture evenly among prepared pan holes. Sprinkle each with remaining cheese and 1 teaspoon of seed mix over each muffin. Bake for 30 minutes or until golden and firm to touch. Stand in pan for 5 minutes. Transfer to a wire rack to cool. Serve.

RHUBARB BRAN MUFFINS

INGREDIENTS

- 1 cup oat bran
- 3/4 cup boiling water, plus 1 tbsp extra
- 6 stalks rhubarb, trimmed, chopped
- 2/3 cup Coles brand brown sugar
- 1 egg, lightly beaten
- 2 tbsp vegetable oil
- 1 cup self-raising flour, sifted
- 1/4 cup milk

METHOD

Step 1: Combine oat bran and boiling water in a bowl. Set aside for 20 mins or until water is absorbed.

Step 2: Preheat oven to 200C or 180C fan. Line 10 holes of a 1/3-cup capacity muffin pan with paper cases.

Step 3: Place rhubarb, 1 tablespoon brown sugar and extra boiling water in a bowl. Toss to combine.

Step 4: Whisk remaining brown sugar, egg and oil in a large bowl. Stir in bran mixture until smooth. Add flour, milk and half the chopped rhubarb. Stir until just combined. Spoon into paper cases.

Step 5: Scatter over remaining rhubarb and bake for 25-30 mins until muffins spring back when lightly touched. Cool on a wire rack.

BROC TOTS

INGREDIENTS

- 250g broccoli florets (you'll need a 350g head)
- 3/4 cup (60g) panko breadcrumbs
- 3/4 cup (90g) shredded tasty cheddar
- 2 spring onions, finely chopped
- 1 Coles Australian Free Range Egg, lightly whisked
- 20g butter, melted
- Tzatziki, to serve

METHOD

Step 1: Preheat oven to 230°C (210°C fan-forced). Line a baking tray with baking paper.

Step 2: In a large pot of salted boiling water, cook broccoli for 3 mins or until tender. Drain and transfer to a plate lined with paper towel. Set aside to cool.

Step 3: Finely chop broccoli (there should be 2 cups chopped broccoli). In a medium bowl, combine broccoli, breadcrumbs, cheddar, spring onions, egg and melted butter. Using a wooden spoon, mix until very well combined. Transfer mixture to the fridge and chill for 20 mins.

Step 4: Roll tablespoonfuls of broccoli mixture into balls. Using moistened hands, press balls into cylinder shapes. Place onto the prepared baking tray.

Step 5: Bake for 10 mins or until undersides are golden. Flip over (some melted cheese may seep out, causing them to stick – gently coax these ones from the baking paper). After flipping, cook for 5 mins longer or until bottoms are golden. Cool slightly then serve with tzatziki.

SALMON BALLS WITH LEMON SAUCE

INGREDIENTS

- 250g Desiree potatoes, cut into 3cm pieces
- 2 x 200g cans salmon, drained, flaked
- 2 lemons, rind finely grated, juiced
- 1/4 cup dill leaves, chopped
- 1 cup dried breadcrumbs
- Olive oil cooking spray
- 3/4 cup sour cream

METHOD

Step 1: Place potatoes into a saucepan. Cover with cold water. Bring to the boil over high heat. Reduce heat to low. Simmer for 15 minutes or until tender. Drain well. Return to saucepan. Mash. Transfer to a bowl. Cool.

Step 2: Preheat oven to 200°C. Line a baking tray with baking paper. Add salmon, half the lemon rind, 1/4 cup of lemon juice, 2 tablespoons of dill, and salt and pepper to potato. Mix well to combine.

Step 3: Place breadcrumbs onto a plate. Using wet hands, roll tablespoonfuls of salmon mixture into balls. Roll in breadcrumbs.

Step 4: Place onto prepared tray. Spray with oil. Bake for 15 minutes or until golden.

Step 5: Mix together sour cream, remaining dill, lemon rind, lemon juice, and salt and pepper. Serve with salmon balls.

PARMESAN CAULIFLOWER

Preparation time: 15 minutes

Cooking time: 15 minutes

Servings: 5

Ingredients:

- 8 cups small cauliflower florets (about 1¼lbs/567g)
- 3 tablespoons olive oil
- 1 teaspoon garlic powder
- ½ teaspoon salt
- ½ teaspoon turmeric
- ¼ cup shredded Parmesan cheese

Directions

- In a bowl, combine the cauliflower florets, olive oil, garlic powder, salt, turmeric, and toss to coat. Transfer to the air fryer basket.

- Select "Air Fry" temperature to 390 degrees Fahrenheit (199 degrees Celsius), and set time to 15 minutes.
- After 5 minutes, remove, then stir the cauliflower florets. Return to the oven and continue cooking.
- After 6 minutes, remove and stir the cauliflower again. Return and cook again for 4 minutes. The cauliflower florets should be crisp-tender.
- Sprinkle with the shredded Parmesan cheese and toss well. Serve warm.

Nutrition:

- Calories 58
- Carbohydrates 6g
- Fat 3g
- Protein 3g

BEEF AND MANGO SKEWERS

Preparation time: 10 minutes

Cooking time: 5 minutes

Servings: 4

Ingredients:

- 2 tablespoons balsamic vinegar
- 1 tablespoon olive oil
- 1 tablespoon honey
- ½ teaspoon dried marjoram
- A pinch of salt
- Freshly ground black pepper
- 1 mango
- ¾ pound beef sirloin (cut into 1-inch cubes)

Directions

- Put the meat cubes in a medium bowl and add the balsamic vinegar, olive oil, honey, marjoram, salt, and pepper. Mix well and then massage the marinade into the meat with your hands. Set aside.
- To prepare the mango, leave it last and cut the skin with a sharp blade.
- Then gently cut around the oval pit to remove the pulp. Cut the mango into 1-inch cubes.
- The metal wire skewers alternate with three cubes of meat and two cubes of mango.
- Bake the skewers in the skillet for 4 to 7 minutes or until the meat is browned and at least 145 degrees Fahrenheit.

Nutrition:

- Calories 242
- Total Fat 9g
- Saturated Fat 3g
- Cholesterol 76mg
- Sodium 96mg
- Carbohydrates 13g
- Fiber 1g
- Protein 26g

SPICY KALE CHIPS WITH YOGURT SAUCE

Preparation time: 10 minutes

Cooking time: 5 minutes

Servings: 4

Ingredients:

- 1 cup Greek yogurt
- 3 tablespoons lemon juice
- 2 tablespoons honey mustard
- ½ teaspoon dried oregano
- 1 bunch curly kale
- 2 tablespoons olive oil
- 1/2 teaspoon salt
- 1/8 Teaspoon pepper

Preparation

- In a bowl, add together the yogurt, lemon juice, honey mustard, and oregano and set aside.
- Remove the stems and ribs from the cabbage with a sharp knife. Cut the leaves into 2 to 3-inch pieces.
- Toss the cabbage with olive oil, salt, and pepper. Massage the oil with your hands.
- Fry the kale in batches until crisp, about 5 minutes, shaking the basket once during cooking. Serve with yogurt sauce.

Nutrition:

- Calories 154
- Total Fat 8g
- Saturated Fat 2g
- Cholesterol 3mg
- Sodium 378mg
- Carbohydrates 13g
- Fiber 1g
- Protein 8g

CHICKEN CHIMICHANGAS

INGREDIENTS

- 485g Old El Paso Burrito Kit
- 4 small chicken breast fillets
- 1 small red capsicum, deseeded, finely chopped
- 3 green shallots, chopped
- 250g pkt cauliflower rice
- 140g (1/2 cup) refried beans
- 100g (1 cup) grated 4 cheese melt
- Sour cream, to serve (optional)
- Lime wedges, to serve

METHOD

Step 1: Preheat oven to 180°C/160°C fan forced. Preheat the oven grill on high. Line a baking tray with baking paper. Place the chicken in a large snap-lock bag. Add the burrito spice mix. Seal and shake to coat. Transfer the chicken to a lightly greased baking tray. Spray with olive oil. Cook under the grill for 3-4 minutes each side, until golden and cooked through. Remove and cover with foil. Set aside.

Step 2: Meanwhile, heat a non-stick frying pan over medium heat. Lightly spray with oil. Cook the capsicum and shallot, stirring, for 2-3 minutes or until softened slightly. Add the cauliflower rice and cook, stirring, for 3-4 minutes, until just tender. Remove from the heat. Season. Allow to cool. Divide into 8 portions.

Step 3: Thinly slice the chicken. Heat 2 tortillas in the microwave on High for 20-30 seconds to soften. Spread the centre of each tortilla with 1 tablespoon refried beans. Top with some cheese, chicken and cauliflower rice mixture. Fold over the tortilla to make a parcel. Place, seam side down, on the prepared tray. Repeat with the remaining tortillas and filling. Bake the chimichangas for 15-20 minutes or until lightly golden and warmed through. (If you prefer soft chimichangas, wrap in foil before baking.) Serve the chimichangas with sour cream, mild Mexican salsa and lime wedges.

CHEESY ROASTED JALAPEÑO POPPERS

Preparation time: 15 minutes

Cooking time: 15 minutes

Servings: 8

Ingredients:

- 6oz (170g) cream cheese, at room temperature
- 4oz (113g) shredded Cheddar cheese
- 1 teaspoon chili powder
- 12 large jalapeño peppers, deseeded and sliced in half lengthwise
- 2 slices cooked bacon, chopped
- ¼ cup panko bread crumbs
- 1 tablespoon butter, melted

Directions

- Mix the cream cheese, Cheddar cheese, and chili powder in a medium bowl. Spoon the cheese mixture into the jalapeño halves and arrange them in the baking pan.
- In a small bowl, stir the bacon, bread crumbs, and butter. Sprinkle the mixture over the jalapeño halves.
- Roast, then temperature to 375 degrees Fahrenheit (190 degrees Celsius) and set time to 15 minutes.
- Remove, then let the poppers cool for 5 minutes before serving.

Nutrition:

- Calories 280
- Carbohydrates 24g
- Fat 19g
- Protein 4g

AIR FRIED LEMON-PEPPER WINGS

Preparation time: 5 minutes

Cooking time: 24 minutes

Servings: 10

Ingredients:

- 2 pounds (907g) chicken wings
- 4½ teaspoons salt-free lemon pepper seasoning
- 1½ teaspoons baking powder
- 1½ teaspoons kosher salt

Directions

- Toss all the fixings until well coated in a large bowl. Put the
  wings in the air fryer basket, making sure they don't crowd
  each other too much.

- Select "Air Fry" set temperature to 375 degrees Fahrenheit (190 degrees Celsius) and set time to 24 minutes.
- After 12 minutes, remove and turn the wings over. Return to the oven to continue cooking until done. Let rest for 5 minutes before serving.

Nutrition:

- Calories 110
- Carbohydrates 0g
- Fat 9g
- Protein 8g

COOKIES RECIPES

CUTE CRITTER COOKIES

INGREDIENTS

- 12 digestive biscuits
- 1 cup (160g) icing sugar mixture
- 50g pkt Nestlé Smarties
- Chocolate writing icing
- Red liquid food colouring
- 20g pkt Coles Funny Face Icing Figurines
- Brown Mars M&M's Minis

METHOD

Step 1: Place the digestive biscuits on a serving plate.

Step 2: Place the icing sugar in a bowl. Stir in enough cold water to make a smooth paste.

Step 3: To make butterflies and caterpillars, spread two-thirds of the icing over 8 of the biscuits. Decorate with Smarties and writing icing. Set aside to set.

Step 4: To make ladybirds, tint the remaining icing red. Spread red icing over the remaining biscuits. Decorate with Funny Face Icing Figurine eyes, writing icing and M&M's. Set aside to set.

ALMOND AND CHERRY COOKIES

INGREDIENTS

- 160g butter, softened
- 1/2 cup (110g) Coles Caster Sugar
- 2 Coles Australian Free Range Eggs
- 1 tsp almond essence
- 1/4 tsp pink liquid food colouring
- 2 cups (300g) plain flour
- 1 cup (120g) almond meal
- 200g pkt red glacé cherries, coarsely chopped
- 1/2 cup (70g) pistachios, coarsely chopped
- 1/2 cup (40g) desiccated coconut

METHOD

Step 1: Line 2 baking trays with baking paper. Use an electric mixer to beat the butter, sugar, eggs, almond essence and food colouring in a large bowl until well combined. Stir in the flour and almond meal. Add the cherry and pistachio and stir until well combined.

Step 2: Turn the dough onto a lightly floured surface and gently knead until smooth. Divide into 2 even portions. Roll each portion into a 22cm log. Place the coconut on a plate. Roll the logs in coconut to coat. Cover with plastic wrap. Place in the fridge for 30 mins to chill.

Step 3: Preheat oven to 160°C. Cut the logs into 1cm-thick slices. Place the slices on the trays, about 3cm apart. Bake for 20 mins or until golden and firm. Transfer the cookies to a wire rack to cool completely.

RECIPE NOTES

Allow for cooling and 30 minutes chilling time.

SLICE IT RIGHT - For perfectly round slices, chill the log for 30 mins before slicing – too soft and the log won't retain its shape as you cut.

FREEZE THE DOUGH - Freeze in an airtight container for up to 3 months. Slice and bake from frozen for 23-25 mins or until golden and firm.

BANANA COOKIES

INGREDIENTS

COOKIE DOUGH BASE

- 125g salted butter, softened
- 1/2 cup brown sugar
- 1/4 cup caster sugar
- 1 egg
- 1 cup traditional rolled oats
- 1/2 cup self-raising flour
- 1/2 cup wholemeal self-raising flour

BANANA COOKIES

- 1 ripe banana, mashed
- 1/2 cup roughly chopped banana chips
- 100g dark chocolate, melted

METHOD

Step 1: Using an electric mixer, beat butter and sugars until pale and creamy. Add egg. Beat well to combine. Add oats and flours. Stir with a wooden spoon to combine.

Step 2: Preheat oven to 190°C/170°C fan-forced. Line 2 baking trays with baking paper. Add banana and chips to dough. Stir to combine. Refrigerate for 45 minutes to firm slightly.

Step 3: Roll 2 level tablespoons of mixture into 16 balls. Place onto prepared trays, allowing room for spreading. Using the palm of your hand, slightly flatten to form a 5.5cm round. Bake for 12 to 14 minutes, swapping trays after 10 minutes, or until light golden. Stand cookies on trays for 5 minutes. Transfer to a wire rack to cool.

Step 4: Place cookies on a sheet of baking paper. Spoon chocolate into a snap-lock bag. Snip off one corner. Drizzle chocolate over cookies. Stand until chocolate sets. Serve.

TRASH COOKIES

INGREDIENTS

- 1 1/2 cups plain flour
- 1/2 tsp cream of tartar
- 1/2 tsp bicarbonate of soda
- 3/4 cup caster sugar
- 125g butter, melted, cooled
- 2 tsp vanilla extract
- 1 egg, lightly beaten
- 1/2 cup jelly beans
- 1 1/3 cups mini pretzels
- 1 cup mixed M&M's
- 12.5g sachet Wizz Fizz sherbert

METHOD

Step 1: Preheat oven to 180C/160C fan-forced. Grease 4 large baking trays. Line with baking paper.

Step 2: Sift flour, cream of tartar and bicarbonate of soda into a large bowl. Stir in sugar. Add butter, vanilla and egg. Mix well to combine. Roll level tablespoons of mixture into balls. Flatten each ball into a disc and place on prepared trays, 5cm apart. Top with jelly beans, pretzels and M&M's, pressing to secure.

Step 3: Bake cookies, 2 trays at a time, for 12 to 15 minutes or until just turning golden around the edges. Cool on trays for 5 minutes. Transfer to a wire rack to cool completely. Dust with sherbert. Serve.

RECIPE NOTES

You will need to pile the toppings liberally onto the biscuits, as the biscuits spread a lot during cooking.

MILO THUMBPRINT COOKIES

INGREDIENTS

- 125g butter, softened
- 1 tsp vanilla extract
- 1/2 cup firmly packed brown sugar
- 1 egg
- 1/2 cup Milo
- 1/2 cup almond meal
- 1 1/4 cups plain flour
- 1/4 cup strawberry jam

METHOD

Step 1: Preheat oven to 180C/160C fan-forced. Line 2 large baking trays with baking paper.

Step 2: Using an electric mixer, beat butter, vanilla and sugar in a bowl until light and fluffy. Add egg, beating well to combine. Using a wooden spoon, stir in Milo, almond meal and flour until combined.

Step 3: Using damp hands, roll 2 level tablespoons of mixture into balls. Place balls onto prepared baking trays 6cm apart to allow room for spreading. Flatten slightly. Using your thumb or the back of a spoon, make a 3cm-wide indentation in the centre of each cookie. Fill each hole with 1/2 teaspoon jam.

Step 4: Bake for 15 to 20 minutes, swapping trays after 10 minutes, or until light golden. Using remaining jam, top up holes with another 1/2 teaspoon jam. Cool on trays. Serve.

APRICOT AND PISTACHIO COOKIES

INGREDIENTS

COOKIE DOUGH BASE

- 125g salted butter, softened
- 1/2 cup brown sugar
- 1/4 cup caster sugar
- 1 egg
- 1 cup traditional rolled oats
- 1/2 cup self-raising flour
- 1/2 cup wholemeal self-raising flour

APRICOT AND PISTACHIO COOKIES

- 2 tbsp sunflower kernels
- 1 tbsp white chia seeds
- 1/2 tsp ground cinnamon
- 2 tbsp finely chopped dried apricots

- 2 tbsp finely chopped pistachio kernels

METHOD

Step 1: Using an electric mixer, beat butter and sugars until pale and creamy. Add egg. Beat well to combine. Add oats and flours. Stir with a wooden spoon to combine.

Step 2: Preheat oven to 190°C/170°C fan-forced. Line 2 baking trays with baking paper. Add sunflower kernels, chia seeds and cinnamon to dough. Stir to combine.

Step 3: Roll 2 level tablespoons of mixture into 16 balls. Place onto prepared trays, allowing room for spreading. Using the palm of your hand, slightly flatten to form a 5.5cm round. Top with apricots and pistachios. Bake for 15 minutes, swapping trays after 10 minutes, or until light golden. Stand cookies on trays for 5 minutes. Transfer to a wire rack to cool. Serve.

CHOCOLATE AND COCONUT COOKIES

INGREDIENTS

COOKIE DOUGH BASE

- 125g salted butter, softened
- 1/2 cup brown sugar
- 1/4 cup caster sugar
- 1 egg
- 1 cup traditional rolled oats
- 1/2 cup self-raising flour
- 1/2 cup wholemeal self-raising flour

CHOLOATE AND COCONUT COOKIES

- 1 quantity cookie dough base
- 3/4 cup coconut flakes, roughly chopped
- 2 tbsp dark chocolate chips

METHOD

Step 1: Using an electric mixer, beat butter and sugars until pale and creamy. Add egg. Beat well to combine. Add oats and flours. Stir with a wooden spoon to combine.

Step 2: Preheat oven to 190°C/170°C fan-forced. Line 2 baking trays with baking paper. Add ½ cup coconut to dough. Stir to combine.

Step 3: Roll 2 level tablespoons of mixture into 16 balls. Place onto prepared trays, allowing room for spreading. Using the palm of your hand, slightly flatten to form a 5.5cm round. Top with chocolate chips and remaining coconut. Bake for 15 minutes, swapping trays after 10 minutes, or until light golden. Stand cookies on trays for 5 minutes. Transfer to a wire rack to cool. Serve.

CHOCOLATE CHILLI COOKIES

INGREDIENTS

COOKIE DOUGH BASE

- 125g salted butter, softened
- 1⁄2 cup brown sugar
- 1⁄4 cup caster sugar
- 1 egg
- 1 cup traditional rolled oats
- 1⁄2 cup self-rising flour
- 1⁄2 cup wholemeal self-raising flour

CHOCOLATE CHILLI COOKIES

- 100g dark chocolate, melted
- 1 tsp ground cinnamon
- 1⁄2 tsp vanilla bean paste
- Pinch dried red chilli flakes

METHOD

Step 1: Using an electric mixer, beat butter and sugars until pale and creamy. Add egg. Beat well to combine. Add oats and flours. Stir with a wooden spoon to combine.

Step 2: Preheat oven to 190°C/170°C fan-forced. Line 2 baking trays with baking paper. Add melted chocolate, cinnamon and vanilla to basic dough. Stir to combine.

Step 3: Roll 2 level tablespoons of mixture into 16 balls. Place onto prepared trays, allowing room for spreading. Using the palm of your hand, slightly flatten to form a 5.5cm round. Sprinkle with chilli flakes. Bake for 15 minutes, swapping trays after 10 minutes, or until light golden. Stand cookies on trays for 5 minutes before transferring to a wire rack to cool. Serve.

EASY KITKAT COOKIES

INGREDIENTS

- 2 x 170g blocks Nestlé KitKat
- 225g unsalted butter, softened
- 75g (1/3 cup) caster sugar
- 180ml (3/4 cup) Nestlé Sweetened Condensed Milk
- 300g (2 cups) plain flour
- 1 tsp baking powder
- 200g pkt Nestlé Bakers' Choice Milk Choc Bits
- 2 tbsp Nestlé Bakers' Choice Cocoa Powder

METHOD

Step 1: Preheat oven to 190C/170C fan-forced. Grease and line three large baking trays.

Step 2: Open the blocks of KitKat and chop 10 fingers into thirds (so you have 30 small pieces in total) and set aside. Finely chop remaining fingers.

Step 3: Using an electric mixer, beat butter and sugar until pale and creamy. Beat in sweetened condensed milk. Sift the flour and baking powder together and stir into butter mixture until combined. Stir in milk chic bits and finely chopped KitKat.

Step 4: Spoon 1/3 of the cookie mixture into a bowl and stir in the cocoa powder until combined. Return cocoa mixture to the remaining cookie mixture and mix gently to swirl both mixtures together.

Step 5: Roll level tablespoons of mixture into balls and place, 5cm apart, on prepared trays. Bake for 15 minutes or until golden. Top each hot cookie with a piece of KitKat and press in gently. Set aside to cool. Serve.

CHOCKY ROCK COOKIES

INGREDIENTS

- 125g butter
- 1/2 cup (110g) caster sugar
- 1 Coles Australian Free Range Egg, lightly whisked
- 1 cup (150g) plain flour
- 1/2 tsp baking powder
- 1/2 cup (80g) sultanas
- 2/3 cup (130g) dark chocolate chips
- 1/2 cup (45g) rolled oats
- 2 cups (80g) cornflakes

METHOD

Step 1: Preheat oven to 180°C. Line 2 large baking trays with baking paper. Use an electric mixer to beat the butter and sugar in a large bowl until pale and creamy. Add the egg and beat until well combined. Add the flour and baking powder and stir to combine.

Step 2: Add the sultanas, chocolate chips, oats and half the cornflakes to the flour mixture. Stir to combine.

Step 3: Place the remaining cornflakes in a medium bowl and use a wooden spoon to lightly crush.

Step 4: Roll 1-tbs portions of the sultana mixture into balls, then dip in the crushed cornflakes to lightly coat. Place on the lined trays. Flatten slightly.

Step 5: Bake, swapping the trays halfway through cooking, for 15 mins or until light golden. Transfer to a wire rack to cool completely.

CRANBERRY LEMON COOKIES

INGREDIENTS

COOKIE DOUGH BASE

- 125g salted butter, softened
- 1/2 cup brown sugar
- 1/4 cup caster sugar
- 1 egg
- 1 cup traditional rolled oats
- 1/2 cup self-raising flour
- 1/2 cup wholemeal self-raising flour

CRANBERRY LEMON COOKIES

- 1 tbsp finely grated lemon rind
- 1 tbsp lemon juice
- 1/2 cup finely chopped dried cranberries

METHOD

Step 1: Using an electric mixer, beat butter and sugars until pale and creamy. Add egg. Beat well to combine. Add oats and flours. Stir with a wooden spoon to combine.

Step 2: Preheat oven to 190°C/170°C fan-forced. Line 2 baking trays with baking paper. Add lemon rind and juice and half the cranberries to dough. Stir to combine.

Step 3: Roll 2 level tablespoons of mixture into 16 balls. Place onto prepared trays, allowing room for spreading. Using the palm of your hand, slightly flatten to form a 5.5cm round. Top with remaining cranberries. Bake for 15 minutes, swapping trays after 10 minutes, or until light golden. Stand cookies on trays for 5 minutes. Transfer to a wire rack to cool. Serve.

TAHINI AND HONEY COOKIES

INGREDIENTS

COOKIE DOUGH BASE

- 125g salted butter, softened
- 1/2 cup brown sugar
- 1/4 cup caster sugar
- 1 egg
- 1 cup traditional rolled oats
- 1/2 cup self-raising flour
- 1/2 cup wholemeal self-raising flour

TAHINI AND HONEY COOKIES

- 2 tbsp tahini
- 1 tbsp honey
- 2 tbsp pepitas
- 2 tsp sesame seeds

METHOD

Step 1: Using an electric mixer, beat butter and sugars until pale and creamy. Add egg. Beat well to combine. Add oats and flours. Stir with a wooden spoon to combine.

Step 2: Preheat oven to 190°C/170°C fan-forced. Line 2 baking trays with baking paper. Add tahini and honey to dough. Stir to combine.

Step 3: Roll 2 level tablespoons of mixture into 16 balls. Place onto prepared trays, allowing room for spreading. Using the palm of your hand, slightly flatten to form a 5.5cm round. Sprinkle with pepitas and sesame seeds. Bake for 15 minutes, swapping trays after 10 minutes, or until light golden. Stand cookies on trays for 5 minutes. Transfer to a wire rack to cool. Serve.

CHOC DIPPED FORTUNE COOKIES

INGREDIENTS

- 100 pkt fortune cookies
- 100g white chocolate, melted
- Pink liquid food colouring
- Blue liquid food colouring
- Coles Funfetti Sprinkles, to decorate
- Coles Star Sprinkles, to decorate

METHOD

Step 1: Line a large baking tray with baking paper. Unwrap the cookies and place on the lined tray.

Step 2: Divide the chocolate into 3 bowls. Use food colouring to tint 2 of the chocolate portions pale pink and blue.

Step 3: Working quickly, dip 1 cookie halfway into melted chocolate. Return to tray. Repeat with remaining cookies and chocolate.

Step 4: Sprinkle some of the cookies with the funfetti sprinkles and star sprinkles. Set. Place any remaining chocolate into separate sealable bags. Cut off 1 small corner. Drizzle over some of the cookies. Set.

VEGAN CHOC-CHIP COOKIES

INGREDIENTS

- 110g Nuttelex vegan olive oil spread
- 150g (3/4 cup) coconut sugar
- 1 teaspoon pure vanilla extract
- 235g (11/2 cups) wholemeal spelt flour
- 1 teaspoon ground cinnamon
- 60ml (1/4 cup) unsweetened almond milk
- 80g vegan milk chocolate, chopped

METHOD

Step 1: Preheat oven 180C/160C fan forced. Line a large baking tray with baking paper. Use electric beaters to beat the spread, sugar and vanilla in a bowl until pale and creamy.

Step 2: Sift the flour and cinnamon into the spread mixture. Add the milk and chocolate. Stir until well combined and a soft sticky dough forms.

Step 3: Use slightly wetted hands to roll tablespoonfuls of the mixture into balls. Place on the prepared tray, about 5cm apart. Flatten well with a fork. Bake for 12 minutes or until golden. Transfer to a wire rack to cool completely.

PEANUT BUTTER SANDWICH COOKIES

INGREDIENTS

- 3/4 cup Lakanto Monkfruit Golden Sweetener
- 1/2 cup butter unsalted, melted
- 3/4 cup peanut butter
- 1 whole egg
- 1 1/2 cups coconut flour
- 1 tsp vanilla essence
- 1/4 cup peanut butter (to fill)

METHOD

Step 1: Combine the sweetener and melted butter, peanut butter and lightly beaten egg. Mix well.

Step 2 Gradually add sifted flour and remaining ingredients, mixing thoroughly.

Step 3: Place teaspoons of mixture onto a greased tray, flattening with a fork.

Step 4: Bake for about 12-15 minutes at 160C.

Step 5: Allow to cool before sandwiching with peanut butter. Serve.

SUPER-EASY JELLY COOKIES

INGREDIENTS

- 250g butter, softened
- 1/4 cup caster sugar
- 1 egg
- 2 1/2 cups plain flour
- 85g packet lime-flavoured jelly crystals
- 85g packet raspberry-flavoured jelly crystals
- 85g packet orange-flavoured jelly crystals
- 1/4 cup boiling water

METHOD

Step 1: Using an electric mixer, beat butter and sugar until pale and creamy. Add egg. Beat until combined. Sift flour over butter mixture. Beat until combined. Divide dough into 3 equal portions.

Step 2: Place jelly crystals in 3 separate bowls. Working with one flavour at a time, add 1 tablespoon boiling water. Whisk to combine (crystals will not dissolve completely). Add 1 portion of dough. Stir with a wooden spoon until well combined. Place on a sheet of plastic wrap. Using plastic wrap to avoid dough sticking to your fingers, shape into an 18cm-long log. Repeat with remaining jelly crystals, boiling water and dough to make 3 logs. Freeze for 30 minutes.

Step 3: Preheat oven to 180C/160C fan-forced. Line 3 large baking trays with baking paper.

Step 4: Remove 1 dough log from freezer. Slice log into 1cm-thick rounds. Roll each round into a ball. Place balls, 3cm apart, on one of the prepared trays. Press down slightly with palm of hand. Repeat with remaining dough logs. Bake for 12 minutes or until light golden. Cool on trays for 5 minutes. Transfer to a wire rack to cool completely. Serve.

CRUNCHY NUTTY CORNFLAKE COOKIES

INGREDIENTS

- 125g butter, softened
- 1/3 cup caster sugar
- 1/3 cup firmly packed brown sugar
- 1 teaspoon ground ginger
- 3/4 cup wholemeal self-raising flour
- 1/2 cup self-raising flour
- 1/4 cup milk
- 2 cups cornflakes
- 22 pecans

METHOD

Step 1: Preheat oven to 180C/160C fan-forced. Line 2 large baking trays with baking paper.

Step 2: Using an electric mixer, beat butter, sugars and ginger in a bowl until light and fluffy. Add flours. Beat on low speed until just combined. Add milk. Beat until dough comes together. Using a wooden spoon, stir in cornflakes.

Step 3: Using 1 tablespoon of mixture at a time, roll into balls. Place balls 5cm apart on prepared trays to allow room for spreading. Flatten slightly. Top each with 1 pecan. Bake for 12 to 14 minutes, swapping trays after 8 minutes, or until light golden. Stand for 5 minutes on trays. Transfer to a wire rack to cool. Serve.

BAILEY'S CHOCOLATE CHIP COOKIES

INGREDIENTS

- 125g butter, at room temperature, chopped
- 100g (1/2 cup, firmly packed) brown sugar
- 70g (1/3 cup) caster sugar
- 60ml (1/4 cup) Baileys Irish Cream liqueur
- 1 egg
- 200g (1 1/3 cups) plain flour
- 1 teaspoon bicarbonate of soda
- 1/2 teaspoon table salt
- 290g pkt dark chocolate melts, coarsely chopped

METHOD

Step 1: Preheat oven to 180C/160C fan forced. Line 3 large baking trays with baking paper.

Step 2: Use electric beaters to beat the butter, sugars and liqueur in a small bowl until pale and creamy. Add the egg. Beat until well combined. Transfer the mixture to a large bowl. Sift in the flour, bicarb and salt. Stir until just combined. Add the chocolate. Stir until just combined. Place in the fridge for 1 hour to rest.

Step 3: Use slightly damp hands to roll 1 1/2 tablespoonfuls of the mixture into balls. Place the balls, 6cm apart, on the prepared trays. Use the heel of your hand to slightly flatten the balls.

Step 4: Bake for 12-14 minutes or until light golden. Set aside on trays for 5 minutes to cool slightly before transferring to a wire rack to cool completely. Serve.

SANTA PULL-APART COOKIES

INGREDIENTS

- 125g butter, softened
- 1/2 cup (110g) caster sugar
- 1 Coles Australian Free Range Egg
- 1 1/2 cups (225g) plain flour
- 1 tsp vanilla bean paste
- 1 tsp finely grated orange rind
- 1 tsp almond extract
- Pink liquid food colouring, to tint
- 2 brown sugar coated chocolates
- Red liquid food colouring, to tint

ROYAL ICING

- 2 Coles Australian Free Range Egg whites*
- 2 tsp lemon juice
- 3 cups (480g) pure icing sugar, sifted

- Egg white, extra
- Lemon juice, extra

METHOD

Step 1: Use an electric mixer to beat the butter, sugar and egg in a large bowl until just combined. Add flour, vanilla, orange rind and almond extract. Beat until the mixture just comes together.

Step 2: Turn dough onto a lightly floured surface. Gently knead until smooth. Divide into 2 portions and shape into discs. Cover with plastic wrap and place in the fridge for 30 mins to chill.

Step 3: Preheat oven to 180°C. Roll out the dough on a lightly floured surface until 3mm thick. Cut a 14cm-wide moustache shape, a 4cm x 14cm rectangle, a 14cm x 6.5cm triangle, two 4.5cm discs, two 6.5cm squares and twenty 4cm stars from the dough, rerolling excess. Place shapes on lined baking trays. Cool on the trays.

Step 4: Meanwhile, to make the royal icing, whisk the egg whites and lemon juice in a large bowl. Gradually add the icing sugar, stirring after each addition until smooth, adding more icing sugar if necessary to make a thick paste. Divide into 3 portions.

Step 5: To make the face, tint 1 portion of icing pink with liquid food colouring. Place a little pink icing in a piping bag fitted with a 1mm plain nozzle. Pipe around edges of the squares and 1 disc. Add a little egg white and lemon juice to remaining pink icing. Spoon over the centre of the shapes and spread to the edges. Attach the M&M's for eyes. Set.

Step 6: To make the hat, tint 1 portion of icing red with liquid food colouring. Place a little red icing in a piping bag fitted with a 1mm plain nozzle. Pipe around edges of the triangle. Add a little extra egg white and lemon juice to remaining red icing. Spoon into centre of the triangle and spread to edges. Set.

Step 7: To make the beard and hat trimmings, place a little of remaining portion of icing in a piping bag fitted with a 1mm plain nozzle. Pipe around edges of remaining biscuits. Add a little extra egg white and lemon juice to remaining white icing. Spoon over the shapes and spread to edges. Set. Pipe white icing over some of the white biscuits to decorate. Set.

ROCKY ROAD CAKE MIX COOKIES

INGREDIENTS

- 440g packet Green's Classic Chocolate Cake mix, Icing Mix included
- 70g (1/3 cup) dark choc bits, plus extra, to decorate
- 55g (1/3 cup) salted peanuts, coarsely chopped, plus extra, coarsely chopped, to decorate
- 25g (1/3 cup) shredded coconut, plus extra, to decorate
- 20g (1/3 cup) mini marshmallows, plus extra, to decorate
- 75g Lurpak Butter, melted, cooled
- 1 egg, lightly whisked
- 60ml (1/4 cup) boiling water

METHOD

Step 1: Preheat oven to 180°C/160°C fan forced. Line 2 baking trays with baking paper.

Step 2: Place the packet cake mix in a large bowl. Add the choc bits, peanuts, coconut and marshmallows. Make a well in the centre. Add the butter and egg. Use a spatula to stir until well combined.

Step 3: Roll heaped tablespoonfuls of the mixture into balls. Place on prepared trays, allowing room for spreading. Flatten slightly then bake for 10 minutes. Set aside on trays for 5 minutes to cool slightly before transferring to wire racks to cool completely.

Step 4: Place the icing mix and boiling water in a bowl. Stir until smooth. Drizzle icing over the biscuits. Working quickly, sprinkle with the extra choc bits, peanuts, coconut and marshmallows. Set aside for 15 minutes or until icing is set then serve.

PEAR AND WHITE CHOC MISO COOKIES

INGREDIENTS

- 180g butter, chilled, chopped
- 1 1/2 tbs white miso paste
- 1 cup (220g) brown sugar
- 1/4 cup (55g) caster sugar
- 1 egg
- 1 egg yolk
- 1 cup (150g) plain flour
- 1 cup (160g) wholemeal plain flour
- 1 cup (90g) rolled oats
- 2 tsp baking powder
- 1 small green pear, cored, finely chopped
- 60g dried pears, finely chopped
- 1/3 cup (65g) white choc bits
- Thinly sliced pear, to serve

METHOD

Step 1: Preheat oven to 170°C. Line 2 baking trays with baking paper. Place the butter in a saucepan over high heat. Cook, stirring occasionally, for 2-3 mins or until dark brown. Transfer to a large heatproof bowl with the miso paste and whisk to combine. Set aside to cool completely.

Step 2: Add the combined sugar to the butter mixture in the bowl. Use an electric mixer to beat until pale and creamy. Add the egg and egg yolk and beat for 1-2 mins or until well combined and a little paler in colour. Add the combined flour, oats and baking powder and stir to combine. Add the chopped pear, dried pear and choc bits. Stir to combine.

Step 3: Roll 1/4-cup portions of the mixture into balls and flatten slightly. Top each with 1 pear slice. Place on lined trays, about 5cm apart.

Step 4: Bake, swapping the trays halfway through cooking, for 20-25 mins or until golden brown. Set aside on the trays for 10 mins to cool slightly before transferring to a wire rack to cool completely. Store the cookies in an airtight container at room temperature for up to 3 days.

RECIPE NOTES

Allow for cooling time.

Seasonal swap: This recipe also works well with apple. Simply swap the fresh and dried pear for fresh and dried apple.

CHOCOLATE AND CANDY CANE CRUSH COOKIES

INGREDIENTS

- 250g butter, softened
- 3/4 cup (165g) Coles Caster Sugar
- 3/4 cup (165g) brown sugar
- 1 tsp peppermint essence
- 1 Coles Australian Free Range Egg
- 2 cups (300g) plain flour
- 1/4 cup (25g) cocoa powder
- 1 tsp bicarbonate of soda
- 250g pkt dark choc chips
- 375g pkt white chocolate melts
- 3 peppermint candy canes, crushed

METHOD

Step 1: Preheat oven to 180°C. Line 2 baking trays with baking paper.

Use an electric mixer to beat the butter, caster sugar, brown sugar, peppermint essence and egg in a bowl until light and fluffy.

Step 2: Add flour, cocoa powder and bicarbonate of soda, in 2 batches, stirring after each addition. Stir in choc chips. Roll tablespoonfuls of the dough into balls. (To freeze, see tip in notes.)

Step 3: Place half the balls on lined trays, 5cm apart. Bake for 12 mins or until just firm. Set aside on trays to cool. Repeat with the remaining cookie dough balls.

Step 4: Place white chocolate in a medium heatproof bowl over a saucepan of simmering water (make sure the bowl doesn't touch the water). Stir until the chocolate melts and is smooth.

Step 5: Line a baking tray with baking paper. Dip one-half of each cookie in the chocolate and transfer to the lined baking tray. Sprinkle with the crushed candy canes. Set the cookies aside for 20 mins or until set.

CRUNCHY CHOC-CHIP MICROWAVE COOKIES

INGREDIENTS

- 125g butter, chopped
- 1 teaspoon vanilla extract
- 1 egg, lightly beaten
- 1 1/2 cups plain flour
- 1/3 cup firmly packed brown sugar
- 1/4 cup caster sugar
- 1/4 teaspoon bicarbonate of soda
- Pinch of sea salt flakes
- 3/4 cup CADBURY Baking Dark Chocolate Melts, halved
- 1/2 cup dark chocolate chips

METHOD

Step 1: Place butter in a microwave-safe bowl. Microwave on HIGH (100%) for 30 seconds or until melted. Set aside for 2 to 3 minutes to cool.

Step 2: Stir in vanilla and egg until combined. Stir in our, sugar, bicarbonate of soda and salt until combined. Add chocolate. Stir to combine.

Step 3: Using 2 level tablespoons at a time, roll mixture into balls. Between the palms of your hands, flatten balls slightly. Line a microwave-safe plate with baking paper. Place about 4 cookies on prepared plate, allowing room for spreading. Microwave on HIGH (100%) for 2 minutes to 2 minutes 30 seconds or until cooked, but soft to touch. Stand for 1 minute. Transfer to a wire rack to cool.

Step 4: Repeat process with remaining cookies in 4 batches. Serve (see note).

RECIPE NOTES

Store cookies in an airtight container for up to 2 days. For a soft cookie, serve on the day of making.

DOUBLE CHOC-CHIP KALE COOKIES

INGREDIENTS

- 50g green curly kale leaves (see note)
- 125g butter, softened
- 3/4 cup firmly packed brown sugar
- 1 tsp vanilla extract
- 1 egg
- 1 1/4 cups plain flour
- 1/4 cup cocoa powder
- Pinch salt
- 1/2 tsp bicarbonate of soda
- 300g dark chocolate, chopped

METHOD

Step 1: Preheat oven to 180C/160C fan-forced. Line 2 large baking trays with baking paper.

Step 2: Place kale in a food processor. Process until very finely chopped.

Step 3: Using an electric mixer, beat butter, sugar and vanilla until pale and creamy. Add egg. Beat to combine.

Step 4: Sift flour, cocoa, salt and bicarbonate of soda over butter mixture. Stir until just combined. Add kale and 2/3 of the chocolate. Using hands, knead dough in the bowl until well combined.

Step 5: Using 1 tablespoon of mixture at a time, roll mixture into balls. Place balls, 5cm apart, on prepared trays. Using the heel of your hand, flatten balls slightly. Press remaining chocolate into tops of rounds.

Step 6: Bake, swapping trays after 8 minutes, for 12 minutes or until just firm. Stand on trays for 5 minutes. Transfer to a wire rack to cool completely. Serve.

RECIPE NOTES

50g green curly kale is the leaves of approximately 3 stalks with stems removed and discarded.

MUESLI COOKIES

INGREDIENTS

- 3 cups homemade toasted muesli
- 1/2 cup (75g) plain flour
- 100g butter, melted, cooled
- 1/3 cup honey
- 1 egg, lightly beaten

METHOD

Step 1: Preheat oven to 170°C. Line two baking trays with baking paper. Combine muesli and flour in a bowl. Whisk butter, honey and egg together.

Step 2: Add butter mixture to oats and mix well. Set aside for 15 minutes. Roll spoonfuls of mixture into balls and place on trays, 3cm apart. Flatten.

Step 3: Bake for 10 mins. Swap trays halfway through. Cool for 10 mins transfer to a wire rack. Repeat with remaining mixture.

SNOWFLAKE COOKIES

INGREDIENTS

- 250g butter, at room temperature
- 210g (1 1/3 cups) icing sugar mixture
- 1 tsp vanilla bean paste
- 2 eggs
- 525g (3 1/2 cups) plain flour
- 2 egg whites, lightly whisked
- 110g (1/2 cup) white sugar

EQUIPMENT

Thin ribbon or string, for hanging

METHOD

Step 1: Preheat oven to 170°C. Line 2 baking trays with non-stick baking paper. Use an electric beater to beat the butter and icing sugar in a large bowl until pale and creamy. Add the vanilla paste and beat until well combined. Add the eggs, 1 at a time, beating well after each addition.

Step 2: Sift the flour over the butter mixture and use a round-bladed knife in a cutting motion to mix until the mixture starts to come together. Bring the dough together in the bowl and divide into 2 equal portions.

Step 3: Roll out 1 portion of dough on a sheet of non-stick baking paper until 7mm thick. Use 6cm-diameter and 9.5cm-diameter snowflake-shaped pastry cutters to cut snowflakes from the dough. Transfer to the lined trays. Place in the fridge for 15 minutes or until slightly firm.

Step 4: Lightly brush the biscuits with egg white and sprinkle with half the white sugar. Use a skewer to make a hole in the top of each biscuit.

Step 5: Bake in oven for 8 minutes or until the biscuits are golden underneath. Set aside on the trays for 5 minutes to cool before transferring to a wire rack to cool completely. Repeat with remaining dough, egg white and white sugar.

Step 6: Thread a piece of ribbon or string through the hole in the top of 1 biscuit and knot the ends. Repeat with the remaining biscuits.

RECIPE NOTES

Cut as many biscuits as possible from the first rolling of dough. The dough becomes tougher the more it's handled, so biscuits from subsequent rollings will have a tougher texture.

CHOC-CHIP COOKIE MASH-UP

INGREDIENTS

- 250g butter, softened
- 1 cup firmly packed brown sugar
- 1 cup caster sugar
- 2 eggs
- 2 teaspoons vanilla extract
- 2 2/3 cups plain flour
- 1 teaspoon bicarbonate of soda
- 1/2 teaspoon salt
- 2/3 cup dark chocolate chips
- 2 tablespoons cocoa powder
- 2/3 cup white chocolate chips

METHOD

Step 1: Preheat oven to 180C/160C fan-forced. Line 2 large baking trays with baking paper.

Step 2: Using an electric mixer, beat butter and sugars until thick and pale. Add eggs and vanilla. Beat until combined. Sift over 2 1/2 cups flour, bicarbonate of soda and salt. Stir to combine.

Step 3: Transfer half the mixture to a separate bowl. Add remaining flour and dark chocolate chips to 1 portion. Stir until combined. Add cocoa powder and white chocolate chips to remaining portion. Stir until combined. Refrigerate both portions for 30 minutes or until mixtures firm slightly.

Step 4: Using 1 level tablespoon of dough at a time, roll mixtures into balls and place on 2 large plates. Using 1 vanilla dough ball and 1 chocolate dough ball, press and shape balls together to form a large ball (do not roll together as flavours will merge). Repeat with remaining dough balls.

PEANUT AND CHOC CHIP COOKIE CAKE

INGREDIENTS

- 125g butter
- 1/2 cup (140g) crunchy peanut butter
- 1/2 cup (110g) caster sugar
- 1/2 cup (110g) brown sugar
- 1 Coles Australian Free Range Egg
- 1 tsp vanilla bean paste
- 1 1/2 cups (225g) plain flour
- 1 tsp baking powder
- 1/2 cup (95g) dark choc chips
- 1/2 cup (95g) milk choc chips
- 1/2 cup (95g) white choc chips
- 1/4 cup (35g) salted roasted peanuts
- Chocolate and vanilla ice cream, to serve
- Chocolate topping, to serve

METHOD

Step 1: Line a slow cooker with 3 layers of baking paper, allowing the sides to overhang.

Step 2: Use an electric mixer to beat the butter, peanut butter and combined sugar in a bowl until pale and creamy. Add egg and vanilla. Beat to combine.

Step 3: Add the flour and baking powder to the butter mixture. Stir with a wooden spoon until well combined. Stir in half the combined choc chips.

Step 4: Press the mixture evenly over the base of the prepared slow cooker. Sprinkle over the remaining combined choc chips with the peanuts.

Step 5: Cover and cook for 21/2-3 hours on low or until the edge of the cake is cooked through. Uncover and cook for a further 30 mins on low or until the cake is set. Turn slow cooker off. Leave the cake in slow cooker to cool slightly.

Step 6: Use the paper to transfer the cookie cake to a serving board. Cut into slices. Serve warm with the ice cream and chocolate topping.

COOKIES AND CREAM MIXED BERRY CRUMBLES

INGREDIENTS

- 750g Granny Smith apples, peeled, cored, cut into 3cm pieces
- 1 tablespoon caster sugar
- 2 cups frozen mixed berries
- 2 teaspoons vanilla extract
- 1/3 cup raspberry jam
- Double cream, to serve

COOKIE CRUMBLE TOPPING

- 75g butter, chilled, chopped
- 2 tablespoons plain flour
- 1 tablespoon cocoa powder
- 133g packet original Oreo cookies, roughly crushed
- 1/4 cup skinless hazelnuts, finely chopped
- 60g dark chocolate, finely chopped

METHOD

Step 1: Preheat oven to 180C/160C fan-forced.

Step 2: Place apple and sugar in a medium saucepan over medium-high heat. Stir to combine. Cover. Bring to the boil. Reduce heat to low. Simmer for 8 minutes or until apple just starts to soften. Remove from heat. Stir in berries and vanilla.

Step 3: Make Cookie Crumble Topping. Using fingers, rub butter, flour and cocoa together in a bowl. Add cookie, hazelnut and chocolate. Toss to combine.

Step 4: Spoon apple and berry mixture into 4 x 1-cup-capacity baking dishes. Dollop with jam. Sprinkle with crumble. Bake for 25 minutes or until crumble is golden. Stand for 5 minutes. Serve with cream.

DATE AND CHOC-CHIP COOKIE BARS

INGREDIENTS

- 125g butter, softened
- 1/3 cup firmly packed dark brown sugar
- 1/3 cup caster sugar
- 2 teaspoons vanilla extract
- 2 eggs
- 1 cup wholemeal self-raising flour
- 1 cup plain self-raising flour
- 1/2 cup traditional rolled oats
- 2 tablespoons milk
- 10 fresh medjool dates, pitted, chopped
- 1/2 cup dark chocolate chips

METHOD

Step 1: Preheat oven to 180C/160C fan-forced. Grease a 20cm x

30cm lamington pan. Line base and sides with baking paper, extending paper 3cm above long sides.

Step 2: Using an electric mixer, beat butter, sugars and vanilla in a medium bowl until pale and creamy. Add eggs, 1 at a time, beating until just combined. Stir in flours, oats and milk. Stir in dates and 1/3 cup chocolate chips until just combined.

Step 3: Spread mixture into prepared pan. Sprinkle with remaining chocolate chips. Bake for 25 minutes or until firm to touch and golden brown. Cool completely in pan. Cut into bars. Serve.

SPICED GINGER COOKIES

INGREDIENTS

- 170g butter, softened
- 1 1/4 cups firmly packed brown sugar
- 1 egg
- 1/4 cup golden syrup
- 2 cups plain flour
- 2 teaspoons bicarbonate of soda
- 2 teaspoons ground ginger
- 1 teaspoon ground cinnamon
- 1/4 cup raw caster sugar
- 2 tablespoons sliced glace ginger

METHOD

Step 1: Preheat oven to 170C/150C fan-forced. Line 2 large baking trays with baking paper.

Step 2: Using an electric mixer, beat butter and sugar until light and fluffy. Add egg and golden syrup. Beat until combined. Sift flour, bicarbonate of soda, ginger and cinnamon over butter mixture. Using a wooden spoon, stir until combined and a soft dough forms.

Step 3: Place raw caster sugar in a shallow dish. Roll level tablespoons of mixture into balls. Roll balls in sugar to coat evenly. Place on prepared trays, 5cm apart, to allow room for spreading.

Step 4: Using the palm of your hand, flatten slightly. Lightly press 1 piece of ginger into the top of each cookie. Bake for 15 to 18 minutes, swapping trays halfway, or until light golden. Cool on trays for 5 minutes. Transfer to a wire rack to cool completely. Serve.